Cultural Stud...
and Cultural V...

David Cahan
Lincoln
April 1995

Cultural Studies
and
Cultural Value

JOHN FROW

CLARENDON PRESS · OXFORD
1995

Oxford University Press, Walton Street, Oxford OX2 6DP

Oxford New York
Athens Auckland Bangkok Bombay
Calcutta Cape Town Dar es Salaam Delhi
Florence Hong Kong Istanbul Karachi
Kuala Lumpur Madras Madrid Melbourne
Mexico City Nairobi Paris Singapore
Taipei Tokyo Toronto
and associated companies in
Berlin Ibadan

Oxford is a trade mark of Oxford University Press

Published in the United States
by Oxford University Press Inc., New York

British Library Cataloguing in Publication Data
Data available

Library of Congress Cataloging in Publication Data
Frow, John, 1948–
Cultural studies and cultural value / John Frow.
Includes bibliographical references and index.
1. Culture. 2. Social classes. I. Title.
HM101.F776 1995 306–dc20–94–30667
IBSN 0–19–871127–1
ISBN 0–19–871128–X (pbk)

1 3 5 7 9 10 8 6 4 2

Typeset by Pentacor PLC, High Wycombe, Bucks
Printed in Great Britain
on acid-free paper by
Bookcraft Ltd.,
Midsomer Norton, Bath

for Christine

Acknowledgements

This book has been taking shape for some years now, and its direction and its point have been changing constantly as people have talked to me about it, changed my thinking in one way or another, criticized what I've written, surprised me or illuminated a set of problems for me, worried me about the rhythm of a sentence or the politics of an argument, and forced me again and again to rethink what the book is about and what work it might do in the world. I can't even begin to thank them all. Instead, let me name and thank the small group of friends who have been most closely involved in the writing of the book or who have made particularly cogent criticisms of it: Tony Bennett, Ross Chambers, Terry Eagleton, Anne Freadman, Larry Grossberg, Ian Hunter, Noel King, Alec McHoul, Meaghan Morris, Lesley Stern, and Graeme Turner.

Most of the writing was done while I was at the English Department at the University of Queensland: I am grateful both for institutional support and for the support and friendship of my colleagues and students there. The book was finished, as far as that can ever happen, during a year's leave from the University, for the first half of which I was a fellow at the Center for the Humanities at Wesleyan University; I owe particular thanks to Richard Ohmann for making my stay an intellectually rewarding one.

Versions of some sections of this book have previously been published in *Cultural Studies* and *New Formations*. Parts of the final chapter have been published in *Shakespeare's Books: Contemporary Cultural Politics and the Persistence of Empire*, ed. Philip Mead and Marion Campbell (Melbourne: Melbourne University Press, 1993) and in *Cultural Pluralism*, ed. David Bennett (London: Routledge, 1994). I am grateful to the editors of these journals and books for permission to reprint.

The book was composed on Nota Bene.
Eleanor Frow and Christine Alavi gave my life a centre.

Contents

Introduction

This is a book about the organization of cultural value in the advanced capitalist world. I argue that — for precise historical reasons — there is no longer a stable hierarchy of value (even an inverted one) running from 'high' to 'low' culture, and that 'high' and 'low' culture can no longer, if they ever could, be neatly correlated with a hierarchy of social classes. I seek to situate this transformation in relation to changes in audience structures and to the increased integration of the aesthetic in economic production; and I then try to think seriously about the class of intellectuals, in a very broad sense of that word, since they play a crucial role in the production and circulation of cultural value. In writing this book I have tried to clarify my position in relation to two sets of problems: I want to understand the changed conditions of cultural production and consumption in the postmodern world; and I want to know why, under what conditions, and on what basis I can and do continue to make and to apply judgements of value within this disrupted and uncertain universe of value.

I pose these questions within the framework of the discipline of cultural studies. But that discipline — both as a relatively arbitrary institutional demarcation, and as a set of problems still in the process of being formed and enunciated — is itself a symptom of one of these problems. It therefore becomes part of the work of this book to subject it to a recurrent (though often indirect) questioning.

Cultural studies is the symptom of a problem in so far as, in defining itself by means of a renunciation of the aesthetic concerns of literary or cinematic or art-historical studies, and in adopting some of the rhetoric and some of the founding assumptions, if not the instruments, of the social sciences, it tends to repeat, and so to be caught within, that opposition of fact to value which has always haunted the latter. To refuse the question of value is not, however, to escape it, and it is in this refusal that I locate some of the generative dilemmas of cultural studies.

Of these, the most troubling is the one that concerns the place and performance of cultural analysis itself. The dilemma flows from the methodological necessity of suspending 'personal' judgement, pleasure, and position in the objectification of a cultural terrain. But that moment of suspension, of separation from the object, thereby deprives it of all its interactive force and meaning, since 'culture' is by definition a realm of uses and of circulating energies.

The division of the place of knowledge from its object can be expressed in one of two ways: as a problem about knowledge itself, or as a problem about social groups. But these problems are not distinct. In the first case, the 'problem about knowledge' has to do both with the specialized and arbitrary languages of institutions, and with the specialization of a caste of intellectuals; in the second, it has to do with the interests and privileges of that caste, and with everything that separates it from the world upon which it reflects. Cultural studies has been prolific of attempts to reconcile the division of knowledge, to overcome the split between reflexive knowledge and its others. The characteristic masks in which it performs have been those of the organic intellectual, the fan, the participant observer; or, more deceptively, it has worn the invisible mask of a humanism which supposes the common identity and the common interests of the knower and the known.

But culture is always a matter both of what binds together and of what keeps apart. At its most basic, it is a concept that refers to the means of formation and of identification of social groups. More precisely, as Fredric Jameson argues, it refers to a social group seen as other, or to my own group's ways and customs *as seen by another group*; it is always 'an idea of the Other (even when I reassume it for myself)'.[1] To use the concept is both to suppose and to enforce a distance of perspective and of value.

[1] Fredric Jameson, 'On "Cultural Studies" ', *Social Text*, 34 (1993), 34.

Cultural studies' starting point is an inclusive conception of culture which it derives indirectly from anthropology and which it understands to cover the whole range of practices and representations through which a social group's reality (or realities) is constructed and maintained. It is a conception that radically disables the forms of universalism held by traditional aesthetics. I argue, however, that even when the relativizing implications of this conception are followed through, the attempt to describe the culture of other groups (which is the necessary condition for defining and describing my own culture) continues in most circumstances to rely upon a projection of moral and temporal distance, an ascription of otherness, that betrays the uncertainty of the place from which I speak.

The construction of the Other (I capitalize the word to indicate the making of a mythical One out of many) implicates this place, and although I talk here about particular classes of constructed Other (the category of 'the people' and of popular or 'mass' culture, for example, functioning as the good or bad counterpart of 'high' culture), my interest is ultimately in that position, and that social group, from and for which knowledge of the objectified Other is produced. They cannot be understood separately: there can be no simple contrast of 'their' cultural framework to 'ours', since the former is generated as a knowable object from within 'our' cultural framework. The division between 'us' and 'them' operates as a mirror image — an inversion that tells us only what we want to know about ourselves. But, as Marilyn Strathern argues, there can be no bypassing of this specular relationship in order to step into an unmediated encounter with the Other; the most that we can achieve is 'to utilize the language that belongs to our own [social framework] in order to create a contrast internal to it'.[2] The focus of this book is, accordingly, not on

[2] Marilyn Strathern, *The Gender of the Gift: Problems with Women and Problems with Society in Melanesia* (Berkeley: University of California Press, 1988), 16; cf. Roy Wagner, *The Invention of Culture* (New Jersey: Prentice-Hall, 1975), 10–12, for a parallel argument that, in so far as 'culture' is an *invention*, which occurs 'whenever and wherever some "alien" or "foreign" set of

the reality of the Other but on the circumstances of its construction and on the 'we' who play and are played by this language game. Chapter 3 seeks, specifically, to delimit the social interests of that group with a professional responsibility for the production and reproduction of knowledge; the chapter is a meditation on the broad 'new' class of knowledge workers that includes, but is not limited to, the traditional intelligentsia, and my own biography is of course comprised in this meditation.

The 'problem of value' is, then, the most general theoretical environment within which this book moves.[3] I hope it will become clear that I am not interested in any return to treating it as a problem in aesthetics, nor in dissociating it from its intrication in an industrialized system of aesthetic production. I take the concept of value in the first instance as an effect of social organization; much of my effort is then devoted to qualifying the simplifications and reductions that might be entailed in this move, and in trying to designate an active rather than a derived role for critical judgement. In so far as the link to social structure and process is maintained, however, the 'question of value' is always involved in social struggle and continues to pose urgent political questions.

conventions is brought into relation with one's own', what is invented and worked out is the interests and categories of the fieldworker's or analyst's own understanding and culture.

[3] This 'problem' currently has a journalistic existence as a set of debates around the 'crisis of postmodern culture'; the crisis is, more precisely, that of the status and the canonical force of 'official' culture, and the agenda set by the defenders of cultural orthodoxy is uninteresting to the extent that it can't open up questions of cultural change (for example, the changes wrought by the restructuring of the cultural sphere by television). I have tried to conduct the analysis in this book at a different level — one that is unashamedly 'theoretical', but also one that allows me to work out problems that are very directly personal. As for the practical and pedagogical consequences of the 'crisis', I can do no better here than endorse Gerald Graff's argument that it is only by teaching the *problem* of cultural authority that we can hope to produce a genuinely rigorous knowledge of the workings of texts and textual systems. Gerald Graff, *Beyond the Culture Wars: How Teaching the Conflicts Can Revitalize American Education* (New York: W. W. Norton, 1993).

The major influence on my thinking about this has been Pierre Bourdieu's work on the sociology of symbolic forms. I first encountered a collection of Bourdieu's essays (in a German translation) some twenty years ago when I was a graduate student in Heidelberg, and in one sense this book is no more than a continuing argument with his sociological account of culture — most of the principles of which I accept. Let me briefly outline three sets of problems that arise in the course of this engagement.

The first set of problems has to do with the relations between class and culture. I argue that Bourdieu works with an inadequate conception of class, essentializing it as a coherent structure and setting it in a fixed relation to cultural forms; culture is seen not only as a process of negotiation of class position but as an expression of it. (Bourdieu's account is also curiously silent about gender and race.) At the same time, it is not clear how far the model of a class-based hierarchy of legitimacies is capable of being generalized. The difficulty is not just that the model is limited by the specificity of the organization of cultural value in France, but that the structure of a linear hierarchy itself no longer seems generally applicable (although it may have local relevances). The crucial factor here, I believe, has been the forms of mass audience constructed by and for television — a phenomenon to which Bourdieu pays little attention. At a more general level, this is a question about the changed relations between the domains of 'high' and 'low' culture.

A second set of problems flows from my initial rejection of aestheticizing conceptions of value (that is, conceptions of value as an intrinsic property of texts or objects or practices). I follow Bourdieu in understanding value to be relational and practical, the outcome of processes of negotiation and contestation; I refuse the conclusion (which is at least implicit in much of his work) that the *sole* or the *primary* function of aesthetic texts is that of status-distinction. The problem is not merely that this restriction to a singular function is belied by the multiple uses to which texts are, as a matter of empirical fact, put, but that to conceive of function in this limiting manner is to give up on the possibility of explaining *other* textual functions (pleasure, to name one) in social terms: with the inevitable result that questions of 'intrinsic' aesthetic value return unannounced and uncontrolled.

The third set of problems has to do with the relation between the position from which descriptions of value-systems are generated, and the content of those value-systems. Questions of relationality and relativism tend not to show up as long as the field of value is conceived as an objectified space; they appear only when the position of the analyst is in its turn objectified and fed into the calculation. Since this object is also the subject of analysis, however, and since — I argue — intellectuals have interests and 'tastes' which, like everyone else's, are shaped by their class position, such a move inevitably unsettles the coherence of the field. It is, of course, for just this reason that this move is so difficult to make. In its absence, however, descriptive relativism empties out precisely those processes of negotiation, contestation, and discrimination that are constitutive of cultural practice, replacing them with a sort of pluralist formalism according to which all domains are taken to be of equal value. Now, it may well be that such a formalism is a crucial *starting point*, since it brackets off the presumed universality of class-specific values; it ends up, however, positing theoretical judgement as quite separate from the sorts of judgement made within the described domains of value, and it obscures the really difficult questions raised by sociological relativism: questions about my occupation of a position and the positional framework of my knowledge.

This is not to argue that 'we' *should* be committed to any one regime of value (either 'high' or 'low'), but it is to say that the question of 'our' insertion into the field of value is crucial, and that this is an institutional, not a personal question. When it is excluded, the process of constructing the field of value comes to be governed by largely implicit assumptions. In cultural studies, for example, the reaction against the privileging of high culture (and the class values it has traditionally carried) has led to a kind of inversion, in which certain *élite* popular cultural forms have been privileged, while other popular forms — 'the easy listener and light reader and Andrew Lloyd Webber fan',[4] for example — are not. This book does not seek to answer any of these questions, but it does seek to lay them out as conceptual problems, and thereby to theorize the position and possibility of enunciation of this analysis.

I understand this book as making an indirect contribution to the critique of some of the foundational categories of cultural studies — culture, class, community, value, the popular, representation. It does not constitute a systematic analysis, however. Rather than producing a frontal critique, I explore some alternative genealogies and analyse the configuration of some of the central terms in cultural studies' preferred problematic.

Cultural studies has always defined itself as an antidiscipline, and even if we take this with a grain of salt, as a self-validating claim, it remains true that it doesn't have the sort of secure definition of its object that would give it the thematic coherence and the sense of a progressive accumulation of knowledge that most established disciplines see, rightly or wrongly, as underlying their claim to produce and to control valid knowledges.[5] Cultural studies exists in a state of productive uncertainty about its status as a discipline. Nevertheless, given its present institutional consolidation, it seems to me important to think carefully about the problems and categories with which it works, since, despite the fact that the development of cultural studies has been repeatedly punctuated by reflection upon its own institutional history, it has in fact been characterized by the poverty of its theoretical reflection. The central 'anthropological' version of the concept of culture, in particular, is a serious embarrassment, in so far as cultural studies has failed seriously to engage with its relation to the traditions of

---

[4] Simon Frith, 'The Good, the Bad, and the Indifferent: Defending Popular Culture from the Populists', *Diacritics*, 21: 4 (1991), 104.

[5] On the concept of discipline of knowledge, cf. my essay 'Discipline and Discipleship', *Textual Practice*, 2: 3 (1988), 307–23.

theoretical and methodological reflection in cultural anthropology and ethnography.

The main line of filiation here is to Raymond Williams's various reworkings of the concept of culture, which draw on two traditions of work: first, on the Marxist theorization of superstructures, and especially on a long history of resistance within Marxism to deterministic readings of that metaphor; second, on an even longer tradition, extending from Herder to Leavis, of theorization of cultures as particularized expressions of the coherence of organic communities.

Williams's most sustained and persuasive account of the concept is formulated in the chapter on 'The Analysis of Culture' in *The Long Revolution*. In his preferred 'social' definition, the term culture 'is a description of a particular way of life, which expresses certain meanings and values not only in art and learning but also in institutions and ordinary behaviour. The analysis of culture, from such a definition, is the clarification of the meanings and values implicit and explicit in a particular way of life, a particular culture.'[6]

Now, something curious happens in these two sentences: culture both *is* the 'way of life' and is the 'meanings and values' *in* that way of life; the 'way of life' and the 'culture' are at once identical and in an expressive relation based on some ontological distinction between them. In this respect the concept of culture is very like Lukács's concept of 'forms', which similarly both holds apart and runs together aesthetic form and the 'forms of life'.[7] It is because of this fusion that

[6] Raymond Williams, *The Long Revolution*, rev. edn. (1961; repr. New York: Harper and Row, 1966), 41. Further references are incorporated in the text.

[7] Georg Lukács, *Soul and Form*, trans. Anna Bostock (Cambridge, Mass.: MIT Press, 1974). The same conceptual pattern in which 'culture' is both opposed (as expressive form) to some anterior domain and simultaneously occupies both sides of the opposition extends into the work of the Centre for Contemporary Cultural Studies. In the introduction to *Resistance through Rituals*, for example, the concept of culture is said to refer to 'the way the social relations of a group are structured and shaped: but it is also the way those shapes are experienced, understood and interpreted'. John Clarke, Stuart Hall, Tony Jefferson, and Brian Roberts, 'Subcultures, Cultures and Class: A Theoretical Overview', in Stuart Hall and Tony Jefferson (eds.), *Resistance through Rituals: Youth Subcultures in Post-War Britain* (London: HarperCollins, 1976), 11.

'culture' can then be taken by Williams to include 'the organization of production, the structure of the family, the structure of institutions which express or govern social relationships, the characteristic forms through which members of the society communicate' (p. 42).

The problem that arises when the concept is taken to be coextensive with the whole realm of meaningful structures and actions is that it then becomes so inclusive as to lose any structure of its own. There are parallel problems with some of the more absolute accounts of culture in anthropology. Marshall Sahlins's *Culture and Practical Reason* is perhaps the most influential example.

Sahlins argues that much of anthropology involves the attempt to synthesize an analytic segmentation modelled on the institutional autonomy of the economic sphere in modern societies, and that this segmentation of the social into material or instrumental reason, on the one hand, and symbolic reason or 'culture' on the other, cannot appropriately be applied to 'primitive' social orders — or, indeed, even to our own. For the function and meaning of material forces is always determined by and within a given cultural scheme. In this understanding

it is not that the material forces and constraints are left out of account, or that they have no real effects on cultural order. It is that the nature of the effects cannot be read from the nature of the forces, for the material effects depend on their cultural encompassment. The very form of social existence of material force is determined by its integration in the cultural system. The force may then be significant — but significance, precisely, is a symbolic quality. At the same time, this symbolic scheme is not itself the mode of expression of an instrumental logic, for in fact there is no other logic in the sense of a meaningful order save that imposed by culture on the instrumental process.[8]

Now, the reasons for refusing the sorts of unilinear determinism associated with the derivation of the symbolic from some more constraining domain of structure

[8] Marshall Sahlins, *Culture and Practical Reason* (Chicago: Chicago University Press, 1976), 206.

(production, practical reason, the material) are well known; but if this refusal entails the loss both of differentiation and of determinacy in favour of an all-embracing totality, then the theoretical gain is dubious. If the concept of culture says everything then it says nothing.

Moreover, as Ian Hunter has argued, Williams's conception of culture has a strongly normative basis. The description of culture as a 'whole way of life', far from delimiting a restricted field of practices, sets up the mode of totality that makes possible the ultimate reconciliation of 'man's' divided being. Instead of delivering 'an account of the social formation of cultural attributes', Williams delivers the narrative 'of their historical unfolding from or towards a "complete" form'.[9] This is to say that the idea of culture tends to repress the specific apparatuses, institutions, and techniques through which subjectivity is formed. When Williams speaks of human evolution as moving towards a 'general human culture' that 'can only become active within particular societies, being shaped, as it does so, by more local and temporary systems' (p. 43), he is both attempting to specify historically the workings of this general culture and positing that it *precedes* any historically specific cultural techniques and institutions. By the same token, the recurrent concept of 'lived experience' is counterposed to all forms of mediation (this is perhaps the reason why in *Marxism and Literature* Williams misunderstands the concept of semiotic code to mean encrypting),[10] or else mediation is seen as part of a process of historical decline (the electronic media work as a second-best substitute for direct human presence).[11]

[9] Ian Hunter, *Culture and Government: The Emergence of Literary Education* (London: Macmillan, 1988), 84; further references will be incorporated in the text. Cf. also Ian Hunter, 'Setting Limits to Culture', *New Formations*, 4 (1988), 103–23.

[10] Raymond Williams, *Marxism and Literature* (Oxford: Oxford University Press, 1977), 169.

[11] Thus modern communication systems are a 'kind of substitute for directly discoverable and transitive relations to the world'. Raymond Williams, *The Country and the City* (New York: Oxford University Press, 1973), 295–6.

Finally, the concept of culture in Williams's work rests, as both Robert Young and Paul Gilroy have argued, on a notion of the experientially established closure of a 'community' which has dangerous connotations of cultural purity. To speak of the English as inhabiting 'rooted settlements' articulated by 'lived and formed identities'[12] is to speak the language of sameness and exclusion rather than of difference and hybridity. Williams's 'culture' can only with difficulty be thought as the creolized and hybrid thing it is.[13]

If the notion of culture as *national* culture — the sense it so often carries (if only in a virtual form) in the work of Williams or of E. P. Thompson — was to prove untenable in the development of the Birmingham School tradition, the figure of an organic link between a community and its expressive culture nevertheless persisted there, at first in the concept of a distinctive working-class culture, but then more influentially in the notion of the subculture, a term that designates the tightly knit identity of a social group bonded above all by a restricted and highly loaded choice of stylistic markers. It is this that makes it an ideal analytic object for this newly emergent discipline: that the principle of bonding and exclusion is not so much the familiar demographic variables of class, region, or even ethnicity — although age remains crucial — as it is cultural choice itself. In Phil Cohen's influential essay 'Subcultural Conflict and Working-Class Community' the emphasis is firmly on the relation between youth subculture and its 'parent' (i.e., class) culture, and in

[12] Raymond Williams, *Towards 2000* (Harmondsworth: Penguin, 1983), cited in Paul Gilroy, *'There Ain't No Black in the Union Jack': The Cultural Politics of Race and Nation* (London: Hutchinson, 1987), 50. Cf. Robert Young, 'The Politics of "The Politics of Literary Theory"', *Oxford Literary Review*, 10 (1988), 155.

[13] In case the example of Williams should seem irrelevant to contemporary practice in cultural studies, it is perhaps worth pointing to Paul Willis's recent celebration, in a kind of inverted Leavisism, of a normatively conceived 'living common culture' uncontaminated by 'institutionalization' or by any interest in 'the merely formal features of art'. Cf. Paul Willis, *Common Culture: Symbolic Work at Play in the Everyday Cultures of the Young* (Milton Keynes: Open University Press, 1990), 2–3. Although Willis is named as the author of this text, it is in fact written by several people.

particular on the way the former seeks to effect a 'magical' resolution to the contradictions of a declining working-class community;[14] Dick Hebdige's *Subculture*, by contrast, shifts the emphasis, especially in the case of punk subculture, away from this socially expressive function and towards the more stylized and reflexive function of representing 'the experience of contradiction itself'.[15] Hebdige's opposition of stylistic innovators to epigonal followers, however, or the opposition mooted in the introduction to *Resistance Through Rituals* between direct peer-group socialization and 'the vicarious peer-group experience provided by the highly visible and widely accessible commercially provided Youth Culture'[16] both promote a normative notion of the authenticity of subcultural expression vis-à-vis the inauthenticity of repetition. 'Style' becomes a figure of the organic relation to a community (or an anti-community), rather than of the simulacral production of authenticity within a highly industrialized fashion system *to which cultural theory has itself significantly contributed*.[17]

The question of an appropriate definition of culture (or, indeed, of whether the concept is worth retaining at all) is not one that I pursue directly in the chapters that follow. But several lines of argument do flow from my concern with this general problem. One has to do with the linkage between culture and class, and I seek to complicate it by invoking the mediation of the institutions of mass education and mass communications. And another has to do with the concept of

---

[14] Phil Cohen, 'Subcultural Conflict and Working-Class Community', in Stuart Hall *et al.* (eds.), *Culture, Media, Language: Working Papers in Cultural Studies, 1972–79* (London: Hutchinson, 1980); this is an abbreviated version of the longer essay with the same title published in 1972 in the *Working Papers in Cultural Studies* series.

[15] Dick Hebdige, *Subculture: The Meaning of Style* (London: Methuen, 1979), 121.

[16] Clarke, Hall, Jefferson, and Roberts, 'Subcultures, Cultures and Class', 52.

[17] Cf. Susan Willis, 'Hardcore: Subculture American Style', *Critical Inquiry*, 19: 2 (1993), 365–83; and Steve Redhead, *The End-of-the-Century Party: Youth and Pop Towards 2000* (Manchester: Manchester University Press, 1990), 25: '"Authentic" subcultures were produced by subcultural theories, not the other way around.'

social identity. To say that the concept of culture refers to the existence of social groups — their formation, their maintenance as coherent entities, their definition against other groups, the constant process of their reformation — is to raise difficult questions about the categories of unity that groups lay claim to, and upon which the theorization of groups often uncritically relies. (It is here, although only tacitly and tangentially, that the argument of this book coincides with the critique of identity and identity politics that informs some of the more interesting recent work in feminist and postcolonial theory.)[18] My concern is to indicate the danger of positing imaginary social unities as the explanatory basis for accounts of cultural texts, and to think of cultures as being processes that divide as much as they bring together.[19]

The book is organized in the following manner.

Until quite recently the realm of aesthetic culture has been built around an opposition between mass-produced 'low' culture and a 'high' culture which was understood to transcend commodity production. The opposition closely reflected distinctions of social class, and even theorists who refused the values attached to this hierarchy tended to accept the social reality of its structure. My first chapter argues that it is now no longer possible to understand aesthetic culture as a unified and hierarchical system of value. But to say this is merely to open up the problem of how to describe contemporary relations of cultural value and authority, and their relation to social power. As a way of exploring this problem I look at Bourdieu's work on cultural distinction, and Certeau's on oppositional cultural practices. Both theorists develop powerful positions which are flawed by their essentialization of the domains of high and popular culture,

[18] Amongst others, cf. Judith Butler, *Gender Trouble: Feminism and the Subversion of Identity* (New York and London: Routledge, 1990); Homi K. Bhabha, *The Location of Culture* (London and New York: Routledge, 1994).

[19] Meaghan Morris and I discuss these issues at more length in our introduction to *Australian Cultural Studies: A Reader* (Sydney: Allen and Unwin, 1993).

by a lack of precision about the correlation of class position with cultural preference, and by a failure to explain the anomalous status of high culture (as the culture of possessors of cultural capital rather than of possessors of economic capital).

These problems become particularly acute when they are applied to the study of popular culture. In the second chapter I examine some of their effects in recent work in cultural studies, and analyse the development of the concept of the popular (as a site of struggle rather than an essential domain) in the work of Ernesto Laclau and Stuart Hall. In rejecting their conceptualization of the popular by analogy with the political opposition between 'the power bloc' and 'the people' I seek to lay the ground for a more differentiated understanding of relations of cultural value.

One of the reasons why the correlation of high culture with the dominant social class doesn't work is because of the specific mediating role played by the intelligentsia (and the fact that so much of high culture is tied to the educational institutions rather than directly to a class). I take up this question from a more explicitly economic and sociological perspective in Chapter 3, analysing the development of systems of production of knowledge in the twentieth century and trying to situate the class of intellectuals within a more general professional-managerial class, or 'knowledge class'. This involves a critique of more traditional conceptions of class, and it means taking literally the concept of cultural capital, as the basis for the formation of this class.

The point of this analysis is to make it possible to reposition the question of the relations between high and low culture in terms of the specificity of a knowledge-based class formation. In theoretical terms this chapter represents an attempt to bring together a Foucauldian account of the role of knowledge in modernity with a (post-)Marxist account of class structures based on the possession of cultural capital. But my account of class is not intended to establish a ladder of social determinations or a new ground of identity. The category of class as I use it undoes the ontological and political unities of gender, race, and ethnicity, and will in its turn be variously undone by them.

If the cultural domain is marked by a disjunction between discrepant realms, then the question of value is posed in a particularly direct way. It is clearly no longer possible to hold on to a universalist aesthetic, but a fully relativist model of aesthetic judgement seems to me equally impossible. If this is so, some crucial pedagogic questions follow: What do we teach? High culture, low culture, or some mix of the two? And what basis can there be for our decision? Do we teach a canon, or expand the canon, or dispense with a canon altogether — and how would this be possible? Are some texts better than others — is it possible for us *not* to believe this, but if we do, what grounds do we have for such a judgement? Is it possible to give a fully descriptive account of value (historical or sociological) — where would that lead us, and where would our own cultural position be found in relation to this description? And who are 'we', who agonize over such questions?

These are the sorts of problems that I see coming out of the shift in the systems of cultural value that has occurred, differently in different cultures, with the move away from a more or less direct correspondence of cultural position with class position. In the final chapter I explore some of these problems, and then take up again the question of the representative role of intellectuals, trying to pose in a rigorous way the question of what is entailed in speaking for others: the question of the enunciative interests of intellectuals.

1

The Social Organization of Culture

Having helped certain contemporary masters at the outset of their careers, the picture-dealer, as a man who believed in progress, had tried to increase his profits, while at the same time maintaining his artistic pretensions. His aim was the emancipation of the arts, the sublime at a popular price. All the Paris luxury trades came under his influence, which was good in small matters, but baneful when larger issues were involved. With his passion for pandering to the public, he led able artists astray, corrupted the strong, exhausted the weak, and bestowed fame on the second-rate, controlling their destinies by means of his connexions and his magazine. Young painters longed to see their works in his window and upholsterers came to him for their patterns.[1]

Thus at its very beginnings the modernist text defines its other. Jacques Arnoux, proprietor of *L'Art Industriel* and a petty capitalist who mass-produces aesthetic objects and disseminates aesthetic mediocrity (he ends up selling religious kitsch), is the embodiment, in Flaubert's *Sentimental Education*, of the commodity production of art. Commodity production is, however, the condition of Flaubert's own activity as a novelist, and it is therefore only in a fairly complex sense that we can say, with Huyssen, that 'mass culture has always been the hidden subtext of the modernist project', and that this project 'constituted itself through a conscious strategy of exclusion, an anxiety of contamination by its other: an increasingly

[1] Gustave Flaubert, *Sentimental Education*, trans. Robert Baldick (Harmondsworth: Penguin, 1964), 50.

consuming and engulfing mass culture'.[2] For this Other is the Same, and the dichotomy is always internal to the modernist work of art.

In this chapter I examine some of the contradictions that arise when aesthetic production splits itself self-consciously into two distinct spheres, in ways that perhaps resemble in microcosm the split between European culture as a whole (an imaginary unity) and its allochronic Others[3] (the Orient, the primitive, the barbaric). This is not an argument for a reversal of these categories, a redemptive overthrow of the hierarchy of values established in this split: for two reasons. The first is that any such reversal preserves intact the binary logic by which the categories are organized. The second is that, in the realm of aesthetic production, this binary logic is from the beginning undermined by the absorption of both 'high' and 'low' culture into commodity production; and my interest is in the complicities that this establishes between them, rather than in what truly holds them apart (and nothing intrinsically does).

There is an informative discussion of that process by which 'high' art comes to define itself against its 'mass' Other in an article by Sandor Radnoti, a former student of Lukács.[4] His argument is that the key feature of the development of art into an autonomous system is that 'high culture and an industrialized low culture aiming at mass production confront each other as split obverse fragments of a conceptual unity, two independent, self-contained, yet inter-related complexes' (p. 32). Although in previous periods (Radnoti cites Aristotle on music) there have been oppositions of various kinds between high and low culture, these have not been derived from a *general* conception of art as a unified domain — a conception which developed only in the second half of the eighteenth century.

[2] Andreas Huyssen, *After the Great Divide: Modernism, Mass Culture, Postmodernism* (Bloomington: Indiana University Press, 1986), pp. 47, vii.

[3] I take the concept of the allochronic from Johannes Fabian, *Time and the Other: How Anthropology Makes Its Object* (New York: Columbia University Press, 1983).

[4] Sandor Radnoti, 'Mass Culture', *Telos*, 48 (Summer 1981), 27–47. Hereafter cited in the text.

The terms in which the emancipation and universalization of the category of art come to be cast are those of a distinction between works founded in freedom and internal necessity, on the one hand, and in unfreedom and external (economic) necessity on the other. The serially produced commodity differs in essence from the self-purposive work of art, which is constituted by the singularity of its origin, and the commodity is by definition excluded from the domain of art. 'Mass'-cultural texts can thus only be thought in terms of their functional relation to the market.

This postulation of two different kinds of relation to commodity production is problematic, however, since it turns the market mechanism into a general explanatory principle that sets off two massive and unified domains against each other. But, says Radnoti,

the assumption of the unity of mass culture is just as much an ideological construction as the absolute generalization of the market, and it is needed precisely for the purposes of another ideological construction: the self-definition of the concept of art. It presents a dystopia, the negative counter-image of a positive utopia. Lowenthal's dictum can be reversed: the counter-concept to art is mass culture. (p. 33)

To the extent that high art is dependent on the concept of mass culture in order to define itself as free and rational, it is possible to say that 'the high art of our age is paradoxically indeed culture-creating art in that it creates its opposite, mass culture. It generates a culture of life in order to articulate itself in tension with it' (p. 37). More precisely, the domain of aesthetic value is constituted by a *double* opposition: between the high and the low, and between the new and the old. Within a modernist aesthetic the *old* and the *low* become equated, as 'most of the new concepts of art push their direct ancestors into the counter-concept, mass culture, the more radically the more they promote their own novelty'. The development of the aesthetic domain over the last hundred and fifty years has thus been predicated on the 'alternation of obsolescence and innovation, and the parallel submergence of formerly high art in the sphere of low art' (p. 35).

This rhythm of alternation can of course be explained as a direct effect or reflection of the rhythm of commodity production (the supplying of an ever more demanding market in novelty), but Radnoti in fact rejects this explanation as reductive. The reality is, he says, that all cultural production is dependent on the market, not simply in an economic sense but in the broader sense that it is in principle subordinated to a common standard of value that allows the difference between cheap and valuable art to be determined. It is dependent upon a *general* and uniform economy of value. Given the impossibility of such an economy, however (since value is a domain of dispute, not of consensus), the self-understanding of modern art can only ever give rise to debate about value, in a constant attempt to maintain its distinction from its mass-cultural other.

This argument seems to me a useful one in that it explains the category of 'mass' (or 'popular') culture not as a sociological given but as, precisely, a category constructed within a historical system. Radnoti doesn't specify the dimensions of this system (he understands it essentially in terms of ideas), but to define its scope adequately you would have to think of it as a complex interrelation of the machinery of aesthetic production and distribution; specific audience formations; the educational apparatus; and the conflicting formations of value that assign a place, or contradictory places, to the texts governed by the system. This is fairly close to Peter Bürger's concept of the *art institution*, and Bürger has argued in similar terms against accepting at face value the categories produced by the institution. The problem with the framework established by the distinction between high and low culture is thus

not so much the judgement (art as social criticism versus the culture industry as affirmation of the bad conditions that prevail), which is probably generally accurate in late-bourgeois society, but the fact that the relation between serious and pulp fiction is barely thematized, precisely because both are assigned to distinct spheres from the very beginning.[5]

And Christa Bürger writes elsewhere that the separation of the study of popular fiction (*Trivialliteratur*) as a more or less independent domain makes it impossible to analyse the prior oppositional constitution of the categories of 'high' and 'low' art.[6]

The starting point for Fredric Jameson's best-known essay on mass culture[7] is likewise the need for reflection on the 'objective status' of that opposition — since 'so often, positions in this field reduce themselves to two mirror-images, and are essentially staged in terms of value' (p. 130). On the one side, the defence of mass culture is made by way of a charge of élitism against high-cultural intellectuals; but given that those making this charge are themselves intellectuals, 'this position has suspicious overtones of the guilt trip' (ibid.). On the other side of the value-antithesis, a position exemplified by the Frankfurt School, mass culture is identified with the commodity and hence with sheer instrumentality — as though high culture somehow managed not to serve any function at all. The difficulty with such a position 'is not its negative and critical apparatus, but rather the positive value on which the latter depends, namely the valorization of traditional modernist high art as the locus of some genuinely critical and subversive, "autonomous" aesthetic function'. To set up modernist high culture in this way as an absolute criterion involves a forgetting of what Adorno,

---

[5] Peter Bürger, *Theory of the Avant-Garde*, trans. Michael Shaw, Foreword by Jochen Schulte-Sasse, Theory and History of Literature, Vol. 4 (Minneapolis: University of Minnesota Press, 1984), p. liii.

[6] Christa Bürger, 'Einleitung: Die Dichotomie von hoher und niederer Literatur. Eine Problemskizze', in Christa Bürger, Peter Bürger, and Jochen Schulte-Sasse (eds.), *Zur Dichotomisierung von hoher und niederer Literatur* (Frankfurt am Main: Suhrkamp, 1982), 13.

[7] Jameson is as unhappy with this term as I am, and puts it in apposition with 'mass audience culture, commercial culture, "popular" culture, the culture industry, as it is variously known'. Fredric Jameson, 'Reification and Utopia in Mass Culture', *Social Text*, 1 (1979), 130; hereafter cited in the text. The terminological difficulty is an index of the difficulty of theorizing the unity of the field.

for example, had well known in his analysis of Schoenberg: 'the historicity, and in particular, the irreversible aging process, of the greatest modernist forms' (p. 133).

What Jameson proposes by way of overcoming the antithetical structure of these arguments is the necessity of rethinking the categories of high and mass culture, not as absolute aesthetic realms but as 'objectively related and dialectically interdependent phenomena' (ibid.). In practice this means reconciling them as antithetical solutions to the *same* 'social and aesthetic situation — the dilemma of a form and of a public' (p. 134).

But this fails to solve the problem, since Jameson's exploration of the 'dialectical opposition and profound structural interrelatedness of modernism and contemporary mass culture' (ibid.) continues to assume the homogeneity of each of these moments: they can be spoken of as great unitary blocks. At the same time, by reducing them to moments of a totality he performs too easy a reconciliation, positing that *general economy* of value that Radnoti spoke of and glossing over the possibility that different (institutionally constituted) cultural domains might have quite distinct problematics of form and of audience. In this respect we might contrast Jameson's dialectic of two moments of the same (two modes of relation to the seriality of the commodity) with Jurij Lotman's postulation of two radically incompatible aesthetics: an aesthetic of identity, based on repetition with variation and improvisation, and characteristic of many forms of folk and popular culture; and an aesthetic of opposition, based on the breaking or absence of expectations and on complication rather than simplification, and characteristic of much modernist art.[8] This model is problematical too, since it universalizes these two aesthetics, but it does have the virtue of suggesting that criteria of valuation may be incommensurable and irreducible, and that it may therefore not be possible

[8] Jurij Lotman, *The Structure of the Artistic Text*, trans. Ronald Vroon, Michigan Slavic Contributions, No. 7 (Ann Arbor: University of Michigan, 1977), 289–93.

to reconcile different structures of aesthetic production and reception within a concept of totality.[9]

But what does the cultural terrain look like if it cannot be seen from a single perspective, and when it is no longer possible to give a privileged status to the texts of high culture? How can we imagine the *dispersal* of cultural authority?

The problem that confronts us is that of formulating a descriptive analysis of the distribution of cultural value without accepting the particular paradigms of value that hold for any given cultural system. I see two major obstacles to this task. The first is that it is at once impossible and undesirable to claim a position of descriptive neutrality, since any description is situated with respect to value. This is not a difficulty that can be overcome by methodological vigilance, but is rather inherent, as the irreducible moment of the political, in all cultural analysis. The second obstacle is the difficulty of dealing with categories which are historically real (i.e. which have real effects in determining the distribution of cultural value between social groups) but which in theoretical terms lack all homogeneity and unity, and lack even an appropriate and generally acceptable designation. The problem is that of describing that general economy of value which is at once the precondition of all modern cultural

[9] Eco takes up this schema in a somewhat more historicized manner. 'The modern criterion for recognizing artistic value', he writes, 'was *novelty*, high information. The pleasurable repetition of an already known pattern was considered, by modern theories of art, typical of Crafts — not of Art — and of industry.' Within the framework of Romantic aesthetics, 'crafts and industry were similar to the correct application of an already known law to a new case. Art, on the contrary . . . corresponded rather to a "scientific revolution": every work of modern art figures out a new law, imposes a *new paradigm*, a new way of looking at the world.' Hence, 'the products of the mass media were equated with the products of industry insofar as they were produced *in series*, and the "serial" production was considered alien to the artistic invention'. The development of a postmodern aesthetics, however, confounds this traditional opposition of value, since it corresponds to a historical period 'for which iteration and repetition seem to dominate the whole world of artistic creativity, and in which it is difficult to distinguish between the repetition of the media and the repetition of the so-called major arts'; blurring this distinction, postmodernism develops an 'aesthetics of seriality'. Umberto Eco, 'Innovation and Repetition: Between Modern and Post-Modern Aesthetics', *Daedalus*, 114: 4 (Fall 1985), 161–6.

production and a fiction which loses its uniform applicability as soon as it is examined.

The reasons for the untenability in the late twentieth century of any categorical distinction between high and low culture (I use these terms as the most neutral I can find)[10] are as follows:

1. High culture is fully absorbed within commodity production. The relation to the market can therefore not be used as a general principle of differentiation between high-cultural and low-cultural products, nor is it any longer possible to employ the traditional value-laden opposition between the disinterested, organic, original, self-governing work of art and the interested, mechanical, formulaic, and commercial mass-cultural text. Works of high culture are now produced in exactly the same serial forms as those of low culture: the paperback book, the record or disk, film, radio, and television (where there now exist specifically high-cultural channels). Within the overall cultural market high culture forms a 'niche' market—but this is also true of many, increasingly differentiated, low cultural products.

2. As high culture has come to occupy this more specialized position (one which is closely tied to the upper levels of the education system), and as at the same time the mass media have come to play an increasingly dominant role in the transmission of cultural values, the relations of cultural authority between the two spheres have significantly shifted. Whereas once, and especially in highly stratified social formations, high culture was unequivocally the culture of the ruling class, this hierarchical structure is no longer the

---

[10] Andrew Ross notes that 'the American use of the term "mass culture" . . . was born of an essentially dystopian Cold War picture of society that was influenced by German social theories about fascism, but it was quickly eschewed in the discourse of the new postwar liberal pluralism. As a more than symbolic refusal of this liberal discourse, "mass culture" became the preferred term of radicals, and so the mandarin Germanic spectre of *Kulturpessimismus* has remained, unfortunately to my mind, to haunt the lexicon of left cultural criticism . . . . On the other hand, the populist tradition of American scholarship has stuck tenaciously by the term "popular culture".' Andrew Ross, *No Respect: Intellectuals and Popular Culture* (New York and London: Routledge, 1989), 233–4 n. 4.

organizing principle of the cultural system. Rather, as Collins argues, it has been replaced by a model

in which those struggles between discourses destabilize the very category of 'the dominant' by asserting multiple, competing hierarchies. In the former type the dominant and resistant can be differentiated with assurance because some kind of supra-discursive formation makes all discourses comparable within the same system. In the latter types of the heteroglot environment, individual forms of discourse construct their own hierarchies that fail to coalesce into one master hierarchy.[11]

The contemporary cultural system 'does not have one centre, or no centre, but multiple, simultaneous centres'.[12]

3. The categories of high and low culture (or their various synonyms), which are structured as a polar opposition, presuppose a more or less direct correlation between culture and class. But the relations of domination and subordination thus expressed have been modified in the twentieth century by the formation of mass audiences which are inclusive rather than exclusive. This seems to be particularly the case with the audience for television, which is structured by the tension between an attempt to construct relatively homogeneous groups of viewers across social classes (the 'core' channels, prime-time viewing, 'spectaculars' of various kinds) and a tendency to extreme differentiation (special interest or minority interest programmes, the range of channels in cable television or deregulated broadcast television). This 'erosion of rigid social categorization'[13] corresponds to the formation

---

[11] Jim Collins, *Uncommon Cultures: Popular Culture and Post-Modernism* (New York and London: Routledge, 1989), 25. Cf. Geoffrey Nowell-Smith, 'Popular Culture', *New Formations*, 2 (Summer 1987), 83: 'The present situation is one in which it is possible to say that there is one culture (albeit with divisions in it) or several cultures (overlapping and rubbing up against each other) but no longer that there are two cultures, high and popular, divided from each other. If pressed, I would probably opt for the view that there is one (multiply divided) culture and that within this culture the dominant position is occupied by forms traditionally designated as popular.'

[12] Ibid. 27.

[13] Morag Schiach, *Discourse on Popular Culture: Class, Gender and History in Cultural Analysis, 1730 to the Present* (Cambridge: Polity Press, 1989), 171. Cf. Tim Rowse, 'The Trouble with Hegemony: Popular Culture and

of a non-class-specific 'popular' grouping, but one that is not structured by its opposition to a 'power bloc'. I'm not assuming that there is no difference between the consumption patterns of different classes, or that (for example) working-class people now have readier access to and interest in 'high' culture; I do argue, however, that for consumers of 'low' culture the sense of illegitimacy or of cultural inferiority that characterized previous regimes of value has now largely dissipated. Indeed, it might make more sense now to argue that, rather than designating definite domains of texts, the terms 'high' and 'low' represent a division that is operative within all cultural domains. Simon Frith accordingly sees the cultural field as being organized by a threefold division between a discourse of 'art' (concerned with the transcendence of body and place), a 'folk' discourse (concerned with integration in a community), and a 'popular' discourse (concerned with cultural experience as heightened pleasure). 'Mass' culture is not the opposite of 'art' but is a way of processing it at different levels, and this means that

the crucial high/low conflict is not that between social classes but that produced by the commercial process itself at *all* 'levels' of cultural expression, in pop as well as classical music, in sports as well as the cinema. High/low thus describes the emergence of consumer elites or cults on the one hand (the bohemian *versus* the conformist), and the tension between artists and their audiences . . . on the other (the modernist and avant-gardist against the orthodox and the mainstream).[14]

4. Finally, the modernist fantasy of self-definition through opposition to a degraded mass culture has become obsolescent, and indeed has been replaced by rather different practices of fusion of or play between high and low genres and traditions. The principle that founds the modernist ethos,

Multiculturalism', *Politics* (Nov. 1985), 71, for an argument that the concept of 'popular culture' cannot be analysed as a coherent category in class terms, since 'one of the possible meanings of "popular culture" is that it constitutes audiences that cut across classes'.

[14] Frith, 'The Good, the Bad, and the Indifferent', 109.

the critique of the cliché, has itself become difficult to sustain,[15] and has in any case been called into question by new modes of relation to seriality and repetition.

The assumption of a global economy of value has meant that the academic study of low culture has tended to be organized in a rigidly antithetical way. On the one hand the tradition of analysis usually identified with the Frankfurt School situated itself explicitly within the modernist self-definition, and defined mass culture essentially in terms of its integration in commodity production. The work of the Frankfurt School is in fact much more various and more complex than it is usually given credit for, but in retrospect there is no doubt that it is badly flawed by its application to low-cultural forms of criteria elaborated for the judgement of high culture, and by its lack of engagement with the specificity of low-cultural texts. Its subsequent influence on American mass culture studies coincided on one side of the political spectrum with a slippage between the concept of 'mass' audiences and the category of the 'totalitarian', a category largely developed for Cold War purposes; and on the other side with analyses, broadly functionalist in their orientation, of the capitalist ownership of the means of mass-cultural production and of American cultural imperialism.

By way of reaction against the contempt for popular culture and its consumers manifested in this tradition, a counter-tradition, growing initially out of folkloric studies, sought to affirm the positive value of popular culture. This reaction has come to inform most contemporary work in cultural studies, but it remains troubled by the antithetical organization of its categories — that is, by the attribution of unitary and opposite functions to the domains of high and low culture. Thus in much recent writing in cultural studies the problem with the

[15] Peter Sloterdijk tells the story of the process by which the bases of Enlightenment criticality come to be revealed as anything other than an impartial commitment to truth and dialogue; come to be revealed, that is, as interest and force. Peter Sloterdijk, *Critique of Cynical Reason*, trans. Michael Eldred, Theory and History of Literature, Vol. 40 (Minneapolis: University of Minnesota Press, 1987), esp. chs. 2 and 3.

opposition of high to low culture has been taken to be the fact that it expresses relations of cultural domination and subordination, and thereby marginalizes popular culture. This approach foregrounds the question of value, and it solves it by reversing the distribution of value between the two poles.

Paradoxically, both the 'pessimistic' and the 'optimistic' traditions of mass-cultural analysis are continuous with those older quests for an authentic popular or folk culture which, as Morag Schiach has demonstrated, have always in practice constructed 'the people' as an idealized category and have then in practice been contemptuous of the 'actually existing' culture of those subordinate social groups for whom middle-class analysts have claimed to speak.[16] There are, however, a number of serious and challenging accounts of the relation between high and low culture, and in the pages that follow I undertake a critical analysis of two of the fullest and theoretically most complex of them, in the work of Pierre Bourdieu and Michel de Certeau.

> Taste classifies, and it classifies the classifier. Social subjects, classified by their classifications, distinguish themselves by the distinctions they make, between the beautiful and the ugly, the distinguished and the vulgar, in which their position in the objective classification is expressed or betrayed.[17]

Pierre Bourdieu's work on the sociology of culture has produced perhaps the strongest case we have — and I think it is an overwhelming case — about the social functions of culture. Starting with the very simplest of questions — Who consumes what kind of culture? And to what effect? — he has produced a complex and meticulously documented demonstration, through a string of books, that the differential use of

[16] Schiach, *Discourse on Popular Culture*, 134.
[17] Pierre Bourdieu, *Distinction: A Social Critique of the Judgment of Taste*, trans. Richard Nice (Cambridge, Mass.: Harvard University Press, 1984), 6. Further references will be given in the text. I have taken this book as the focus of my attention because it is in reality Bourdieu's *summum opus*, recapitulating and often directly citing many of his other studies.

cultural artefacts is fully bound up with the struggle for social power.

The subtitle of his first book in the area of cultural practice, *Un art moyen: Essai sur les usages sociaux de la photographie*, indicates how his interest is focused: he and his collaborators are concerned not with an aesthetics of photography (although, paradoxically, something like this emerges in the book) but with the social uses to which it is put; specifically, they analyse the structures of aesthetic legitimacy in relation to which photographic practices are organized, and the way this relation then produces different conceptions of what photography is or should be — different sets of aesthetic standards — among different classes of practitioners. In a subsequent book, *L'Amour de l'art: Les Musées d'art européens et leur public*, Bourdieu and Alain Darbel reject the assumption that there is a universal and undifferentiated public of the state-run art galleries — that 'everyone' goes — in order to conduct a statistical analysis of who precisely does visit them. What they found was that their public is differentiated along class lines or, more precisely (the difference is important), in terms of levels of education and in terms of cultural aspiration rather than achieved position. The statistics are stark: most working-class people don't go to art galleries, especially when difficult modern art is being exhibited; when they do go they stay for less time than middle-class and upper-class visitors (an average stay of 22, 35, and 47 minutes respectively); and the *musée d'art* reminds them of a church rather than of a library or a store. Experiencing a mixture of hostility and deference, working-class people choose to reject the alienating institutions of legitimate culture, and this means that access to cultural goods 'is the privilege of the cultivated class; but this privilege has all the trappings of legitimacy. In effect, the only ones excluded are those who exclude themselves.'[18]

[18] Pierre Bourdieu and Alain Darbel, *L'Amour de l'art: Les Musées d'art européens et leur public*, 2nd rev. edn. (Paris: Minuit, 1969), 69.

In his major work, *Distinction*, which draws on and synthesizes many of the earlier studies, Bourdieu produced a book with the 'perhaps immoderate ambition of giving a scientific answer to the old questions of Kant's critique of judgement, by seeking in the structure of the social classes the basis of the systems of classification which structure perception of the social world and designate the objects of aesthetic enjoyment' (p. xiv). Using extensive survey material administered over a number of years, Bourdieu sets aesthetic practice in relation to a range of other practices of 'taste', in order to reconstruct the systematic unity of class 'lifestyles', which in turn are generated by that system of 'durable dispositions' he calls the *habitus*. Thus, in addition to being asked about their preferences in painting, music, and photographic themes, the interview subjects were questioned about choices in interior decoration, clothing, food, and politics; and additional evidence is adduced concerning the social differentiation of the body and of language use.[19] In the course of this investigation the book amasses a wealth of material about the distribution of tastes within the system of French culture.

The point of this is not to establish the truism that different classes adopt different lifestyles, but to explore the process by which differences in cultural preference become socially functional. It is a question not of differences in themselves but of the ability of the dominant class to impose the value given to these differences: to impose a recognition of the distinction between 'good' taste and 'vulgar' taste, between legitimate and illegitimate styles. Aesthetic judgements, then, do not obey an autonomous aesthetic logic; they transpose distinctions of class into distinctions of taste, and thereby strengthen the boundaries between classes. But they also assert the right of a ruling class to legitimate domination over other classes. Bourdieu argues this through an economic metaphor: competence in cultural codes constitutes a 'cultural capi-

---

[19] The sociology of language is treated at greater length in Pierre Bourdieu, *Ce que parler veut dire: L'Économie des échanges linguistiques* (Paris: Fayard, 1981).

tal'[20] which is unequally distributed among social classes (although it has the appearance of an innate talent, a 'natural gift').[21] When invested in the exercise of taste, cultural capital yields both 'a profit in distinction, proportionate to the rarity of the means required to appropriate [cultural products], and a profit in legitimacy, the profit par excellence, which consists in the fact of feeling justified in being (what one is), being what it is right to be' (p. 228).

Thus the principle of the pleasure involved in ('high') cultural practice 'lies, in the last analysis, in the denied experience of a social relationship of membership and exclusion' (p. 400). What Bourdieu now calls 'the aesthetic disposition', meaning by this the practices and preferences of the ruling class alone, is dependent upon a distance from need, a 'generalized capacity to neutralize ordinary urgencies and to bracket off practical ends' (p. 54), which links together the owners of economic and cultural capital (and which effectively blurs the difference between the two forms of

---

[20] Bourdieu distinguishes only rather loosely between the concepts of cultural capital and symbolic capital. In his most systematic treatment of the metaphor, 'The Forms of Capital', in *Handbook of Theory and Research for the Sociology of Education*, ed. John G. Richardson (New York: Greenwood, 1986), 241–58 (an essay which also contains an important critique of the limitations of Gary Becker's concept of human capital), he distinguishes only between economic, cultural, and social capital, and this, too, is the major set of terms employed in *Distinction*. In a later essay on social class, Bourdieu defines the 'fundamental social powers' in terms of three types of capital: 'firstly, *economic* capital, in its various kinds; secondly, *cultural* capital or better informational capital, again in its different kinds; and thirdly two forms of capital that are very strongly correlated, *social* capital, which consists of resources based on connections and group membership, and *symbolic* capital, which is the form the different types of capital take once they are perceived and recognized as legitimate' (Pierre Bourdieu, 'What Makes a Social Class? On the Theoretical and Practical Existence of Groups', *Berkeley Journal of Sociology*, XXXII (1987), 4). Thus, although the concept of symbolic capital, which plays the major role in *Outline of a Theory of Practice* (trans. Richard Nice (Cambridge: Cambridge University Press, 1977)), would seem in many respects to be the most general term for non-economic forms of capital, it actually plays a rather restricted role in Bourdieu's later thinking; and I have followed this precedent in using 'cultural capital' as the key term of reference for talking about forms of symbolic competence.

[21] The generation of cultural capital in the schooling system is described in Pierre Bourdieu and J.-C. Passeron, *Reproduction in Education, Society and Culture*, trans. Richard Nice (London: Sage, 1977).

capital). From here the argument proceeds in three stages. First, the aesthetic disposition is defined as conforming to the principles of a Kantian aesthetic which severs the work of art from worldly ends and practical functions. Second, this aesthetic is then equated with an essential class experience: the aesthetic disposition 'presupposes the distance from the world . . . which is the basis of the bourgeois experience of the world' (p. 54). Finally, this correlation is then raised to a more general level: 'position in the classification struggle depends on position in the class structure' (p. 484); the one can be read off from the other.[22]

Two forms of essentialism operate in this argument. The first involves positing a single class 'experience' common to the sociologically quite distinct groups Bourdieu includes in the dominant class. The second posits a single aesthetic logic which corresponds to this experience. Together they suggest that there is an intrinsic logic of cultural practices which matches the intrinsic logic of a unitary ruling-class structure. And one of the effects of this is a binary construction of the concepts of a 'high' and a 'popular' aesthetic understood as something like class languages, fixed and ahistorical class dispositions with a necessary categorical structure.

[22] There is a more mediated version of this model in Bourdieu's frequent practice of reading texts as expressive of the dispositions of authors and then reducing authors to the class positions they represent; for example, 'Differences between works are predisposed to express differences between authors, partly because, in both style and content, they bear the mark of their authors' socially constructed dispositions (that is, their social origins, retranslated as a function of the positions in the field of production which these dispositions played a large part in determining)' (p. 20). More generally, Bourdieu tends to reduce all intellectual practice to the figures of intellectuals and the play of their career interests in a closed intellectual market. He thereby minimizes both the overdetermination of this market by other social forces, and the *ideological* positions — the truth-values — that intellectuals put in play. See Pierre Bourdieu, 'Intellectual Field and Creative Project', in M. Young (ed.), *Knowledge and Control: New Directions for the Sociology of Education* (London: Collier Macmillan, 1971), 161–88; 'Les Fractions de la classe dominante et les modes d'appropriation des œuvres d'art', *Information sur les sciences sociales*, 13: 3 (1974), 7–31; 'The Specificity of the Scientific Field and the Social Conditions of the Progress of Reason', *Social Science Information*, 14: 4 (1975), 19–47; and David Turnbull, 'Pierre Bourdieu and the Blainey Debate', *Arena*, 74 (1986), 133–7.

Whereas the dominant aesthetic is associated with an autotelic formalism, a refusal of practical or ethical function, a refusal of the facile and the vulgar, and with intertextual rather than mimetic modes of reference, the 'popular' aesthetic is defined as having a primarily ethical basis and as subordinating artistic practice to socially regulated functions (for example, working-class people use photography above all for the ritual celebration of family unity).[23] In a rejection of the Kantian prescriptions,

everything takes place as if the 'popular aesthetic' were based on the affirmation of continuity between art and life, which implies the subordination of form to function, or, one might say, on a refusal of the refusal which is the starting point of the high aesthetic, i.e. the clear-cut separation of ordinary dispositions from the specifically aesthetic disposition.   (p. 32)

Thus working-class audiences are (the sense is: inherently) hostile to formal experimentation, and 'their reluctance or refusal springs not just from lack of familiarity but from a deep-rooted demand for participation, which formal experiment systematically disappoints' (pp. 32–3). It is worth noting that the *reasons* for this hostility are not given by Bourdieu's elaborate apparatus of sociological enquiry: he extrapolates them on the basis of a particular construction of working-class experience and of working people's 'deep-rooted demands'. Moreover, the aesthetic he proposes as characteristic of the working class is a conservative realist aesthetic. It could as well be defined in negative terms: as a refusal to consider the intertextual dimension of formal structures, and the social force of this intertextuality; as a lack of critical awareness of the codes through which reality-effects are constructed. And, despite his denunciations of populism, Bourdieu sets up a very conventional opposition — as though of the authentic to the inauthentic — between popular culture and a 'mass market' culture (above all, television) in which

---

[23] Pierre Bourdieu, L. Boltanski, R. Castel, and J.-D. Chamboredon, *Un art moyen: Essai sur les usages sociaux de la photographie* (Paris: Minuit, 1965), 25, 48.

'dispossession of the very intention of determining one's own ends is combined with a more insidious form of recognition of dispossession' (p. 386). The opposition confirms the essentialism by which the image of 'the people' is constructed.[24]

If (like the concepts of elaborated and restricted code for Bernstein) the 'high' and the 'popular' aesthetics work primarily as class languages, they are also conceived in terms of differing orientations to the process of signification. This is expressed as a set towards either the 'form' or the 'content' of the message; and on to this primary opposition is grafted a secondary opposition between the categories 'cold' and 'distant' on the one hand, and 'warm' and 'participatory' on the other. Thus the 'conspicuous formality' of the ruling-class ethos implies

a sort of censorship of the expressive content which explodes in the expressiveness of popular language, and by the same token, a distancing, inherent in the calculated coldness of all formal exploration, a refusal to communicate concealed at the heart of the communication itself, both in an art which takes back and refuses what it seems to deliver and in bourgeois politeness, whose impeccable formalism is a permanent warning against the temptation of familiarity.   (p. 34)

Aesthetic distance — which Bourdieu equates with 'distance' from economic necessity — works 'by displacing the interest from the "content", characters, plot, etc., to the form, to the specifically artistic effects which are only appreciated relationally, through a comparison with other works which is incompatible with immersion in the singularity of the work

---

[24] In a later essay, Bourdieu writes: 'To throw some light on discussions about the "people" and the "popular", one need only bear in mind that the "people" or the "popular" . . . is first of all one of the things at stake in the struggle between intellectuals. The fact of being or feeling authorized to speak about the "people" or of speaking *for* (in both senses of the word) the "people" may constitute, in itself, a force in the struggles within different fields, political, religious, artistic, etc. — a force that is all the greater the weaker the relative autonomy of the field under consideration.' Pierre Bourdieu, 'The Uses of the "People"', *In Other Words: Essays Towards a Reflexive Sociology*, trans. Matthew Adamson (Stanford, Calif.: Stanford University Press, 1990). I can only agree — and wish that Bourdieu had applied the lesson to his own work.

immediately given' (p. 34). A double displacement, then: from the text as it is 'immediately given', and from the immediacy of life on to which the text would otherwise transparently open — since formal complexity 'throws the thing itself into the background and precludes direct communion with the beauty of the world' (p. 43).

The phrasing perhaps indicates that we should take a little readerly distance at this point: that Bourdieu, aware of the extent to which aesthetic arguments are always already inscribed in class positions, is here ironically adopting the language of the popular aesthetic itself. This is doubtless also true of a later sentence arguing that 'often the only escape from ambivalence or indeterminacy towards language is to fall back on what we *can* appreciate, the body rather than words, substance rather than form, an honest face rather than a smooth tongue' (p. 465). And yet whatever irony there is here doesn't modify the congruence of these sentences with Bourdieu's general line of argument. Having written with such force (above all in the *Outline of a Theory of Practice*) against forms of essentialism and substantialism in social theory, Bourdieu falls effortlessly into both when it comes to the aesthetic. It should hardly be necessary to repeat the argument against the form/content dichotomy as Bourdieu employs it, but briefly it is this: that it places content outside the domain of the formal, and that it places the formal outside the domain of content. Coupled in this way, the categories are complicit in a naïve mimeticism rather than being capable of accounting for it.

Part of the problem is that Bourdieu is not interested in giving a detached 'account' of aesthetic codes. Despite the sociological apparatus and despite the commitment to a rigorously scientific relativism, his text is at this point almost explicitly interventionist, working to discount 'aesthetic' experience (understood as primarily an experience of form) and to valorize the directness of the working-class relation to the world. But the implicit supposition that one class stands in a more 'natural', less mediated relation to experience than do other classes is a romantic obfuscation. Bourdieu comes close to taking popular cultural forms as 'authentic' manifestations of working-class life, fully expressive of an autonomous class ethos — and this is made all the easier by the exclusion of 'mass' cultural forms from the definition of the popular. It is as though unified systems of class values were insulated from each other in completely distinct domains.

What gets overlooked here is the question of the relationality of cultural forms. Aesthetic choices are not made in a vacuum: they are made in negative relation to the other *kinds* of objects which could have been chosen, and this involves both the historical sequence to which an object belongs and its position within a synchronic system. To assert a preference (to take a book off the shelf, to tune into a radio station, to look at one picture rather than another) means using an unequally distributed cultural competence to evaluate a text in relation to these interlocking systems of relations. Now, Bourdieu's survey material, and the charts he constructs on the basis of it, do in fact set up rough models of these formations of value (formations which are, as I shall argue, only partly superimposable on social classes). Thus the survey questions on popular singers and on 'classical' music are made to yield various kinds of systemic ranking on a scale of legitimacy and difficulty: across the field, a ranking going from Georges Guétary, Petula Clark, Georges Brassens, and Léo Ferré, to 'The Blue Danube', 'The Sabre Dance', *The Well-Tempered Clavier*, and the 'Concerto for Left Hand'; and within classical music a class-correlated ranking going from *The Well-Tempered Clavier* to the *Rhapsody in Blue* to 'The Blue Danube' (pp. 19–20). But, while recognizing that choices made by the *dominant* class are fully relational, Bourdieu is much more ambivalent about how choices are made within the 'popular' aesthetic. This ambivalence centres on the question of the distribution of cultural competences.

There is a similar argument made in both *L'Amour de l'art* and *Distinction*. It supposes that 'a work of art has meaning and interest only for someone who possesses the cultural competence, that is, the code into which it is encoded'. This competence is crucial for the construction of textual significance: the beholder or listener or reader 'cannot move from the "primary stratum of the meaning we can grasp on the basis of our ordinary experience" to the "stratum of secondary meanings", i.e. the "level of the meaning of what is signified", unless he possesses the concepts which go beyond the sensible properties and which identify the specifically stylistic properties of the work' (pp. 2–3; the phrases quoted are from Panofsky). But one of the effects of the unequal distribution of competences by the schooling system is that members of the dominated classes do tend not to have mastery over the 'specifically aesthetic' codes, and tend to substitute for them a set of borrowed non-aesthetic categories: 'When faced with legitimate works of art, people most lacking the specific competence apply to them the perceptual schemes of their own ethos, the very ones which structure their everyday perception of everyday existence' (p. 44). Ethical and practical judgements are brought to bear on works of art understood as the more or less realistic and unmediated expression of a content.

The earlier form of the argument, in *L'Amour de l'art*, opposes this way of treating the work of art, 'as a simple means of communication transmitting a transcendent meaning [*signification*]', to a properly aesthetic reception, which, rather than detaching the text from any context, relates it to the context of other works of art.[25] The 'popular' aesthetic would thus be not a *different* set of aesthetic codes, but a way of using codes of everyday judgement rather than codes of aesthetic judgement in the appropriation of works of art. And the earlier book suggests that this entails important disadvantages for those deprived of aesthetic competence:

An understanding of the 'expressive' and, if I may use the word, 'physiognomic' qualities of the work is an inferior form of the aesthetic experience because, unable to be sustained, controlled, and corrected by a properly iconological knowledge, it uses a key [*chiffre*] which is neither adequate nor specific.[26]

[25] Bourdieu and Darbel, *L'Amour de l'art*, 73.
[26] Ibid. 81.

The concept of 'deprivation' is itself unsatisfactory because it accepts as given the norms of high culture. The category of cultural disadvantage is, of course, applicable only *on the ground of high culture*. Bourdieu assumes that the legitimacy of this ground is still imposed on the dominated classes; but it may well be the case, particularly since the massive growth of a television culture in which working-class people tend to be fully competent, that high culture, or rather the *prestige* of high culture, has become largely irrelevant to them. (Bourdieu never seeks to *establish* the case for the continuing legitimacy of high culture; he simply assumes it — and he pays little attention to television.) On the other hand, however, the theory of cultural disadvantage does work better, in the framework set by Bourdieu's own account of cultural exclusion and distinction, than his later valorization of the popular aesthetic for its espousal of 'content' and of 'human' values. Again, the value of 'human content' is never explicitly argued for; it is presented only by a double negation, as when, noting that respondents with high levels of cultural capital reject images of a first communion, a sunset, or a landscape as subjects likely to produce a 'beautiful' photograph, Bourdieu suggests that this rejection is motivated by the fact that the images are, 'in Ortega y Gasset's terms, "naively human"' (p. 35). Differing class judgements are described, that is to say, in terms of a differential relation to the photographic 'content', and this content is assumed to have a fixed meaning ('sunset' = 'human'). But of course this is not the case: meanings are not given in texts but are constructed in the relations between texts. The value of the image of a sunset cannot be read off from a photograph, but involves rather the *position* of this image within the system of similar images — a system that possesses a certain statistical frequency and density, a certain sociocultural value. Having a specific competence in this case would mean being able to make an educated guess (literally) about the extent to which the image is culturally saturated and so informationally redundant, a guess about its place within a complex intertextual system.

In the same way, Bourdieu draws too simplistic a conclusion from the strategies of negation that characterize self-conscious artistic production. Thus he writes:

It is scarcely necessary to establish that the work of art is the objectification of a relationship of distinction and that it is thereby explicitly predisposed to bear such a relationship in the most varied contexts. As soon as art becomes self-conscious, in the work of Alberti, for example, as Gombrich demonstrates, it is defined by a negation, a refusal, a renunciation, which is the very basis of the refinement in which a distance is marked from the simple pleasure of the senses and the superficial seductions of gold and ornaments that ensnare the vulgar taste of the Philistines.   (p. 227)

The implication is that this refusal is no more than the translation into the medium of painting of a gesture of snobbery. But this refusal is surely mediated by the function and value of 'sensual' painterly codes in the aesthetic domain, their overdetermination not as 'popular' codes (in the full and naturalizing sense Bourdieu gives the word—'the simple pleasure of the senses') but as codes appropriated and automatized by an art market. Even were Bourdieu correct, however, in assigning a function of exclusion and distinction to artistic practices like those codified by Alberti, his argument would still be wrong because it would still be radically reductive. To write that the 'legitimate culture of class societies' is 'a product of domination predisposed to express or legitimate domination' (p. 228) is to assign a single and exclusive function to cultural practice, and to assume that the work of the text is exhausted in this function. Bourdieu is thereby quite unable to account for the possibility that 'legitimate' works of art might nevertheless be capable of exercising a critical function over and above their other functions.

It is the rigidity with which Bourdieu opposes two formally and functionally autonomous aesthetic universes that constitutes the problem. The immediate correlation of these aesthetic universes with social classes means that cultural forms are understood as non-contradictory expressive unities rather than as sites of tension. Thus it becomes impossible to read, for example, a painting by Goya in terms of contradictions between its functions of cognition and exclusion, or indeed of its changing and potentially contradictory relation to the art market-place; and, conversely, the kind of political analysis that informs the work of, say, Stedman Jones on the music hall, or Willis on working-class counter-school culture, or Sennett and Cobb on the ethos of self-sacrifice in the American working class[27] — work that stresses the ideological and political ambiguity of popular cultural forms — is equally impossible in this account. I stress these *political* deficiencies because much of the recent reception of Bourdieu in English has accepted his account of the popular aesthetic in a quite uncritical manner.[28]

There is, however, a further theoretical problem in Bourdieu's work on culture which raises equally serious questions about the work's political consequences. This is the problem of how Bourdieu theorizes the relation between cultural capital and economic capital — or, to put it differently, the relation between the intelligentsia and the dominant class. Bourdieu defines class in terms of three variables: the volume of capital possessed; the composition of this capital (that is, the relation between economic and cultural capitals); and the change in volume and composition over time (the relation between past and potential trajectories). Within the dominant class 'the structure of the distribution of economic capital is symmetrical and opposite to that of cultural capital' (p. 120), and this means both that the two forms of capital are mutually exclusive, and that — in so far as possession of either is a sufficient criterion for classification in the dominant class — they are in some way

[27] See Gareth Stedman Jones, *Languages of Class: Studies in English Working Class History, 1832–1982* (Cambridge: Cambridge University Press, 1983); Paul Willis, *Learning to Labour: How Working Class Kids Get Working Class Jobs* (Farnborough: Saxon House, 1977); Richard Sennett and Jonathan Cobb, *The Hidden Injuries of Class*, 2nd edn. (New York: Vintage, 1973).

[28] See, for example, Nicholas Garnham and Raymond Williams, 'Pierre Bourdieu and the Sociology of Culture', *Media, Culture and Society*, 23: 3 (1980), 209–23.

mutually convertible. Their structural difference is subordinated to their potential equivalence. But of course this
argument is incomplete: in the first place because the
conversion of capitals can take place only under certain
conditions and at certain restricted levels of the market, and in
the second place because conversion is not reciprocal (it is
possible to convert cultural capital into economic capital, but
not vice versa). In the last instance symbolic and real capital
are not equivalent, and this means that there is a real question
about the class location of intellectuals.

Now, Bourdieu posits that possessors of economic and
cultural capital constitute two asymmetrical (dominant/
dominated) fractions of the 'same' class. It is difficult,
however — given that class is not defined in terms of
functional identity — to know what establishes this sameness
other than the assumed equivalence of the two forms of
capital. Its effect is to bring about a systematically misleading
conflation of the intelligentsia and its culture with the
bourgeoisie and its culture — a conflation that is entirely the
consequence of the initial methodological decision.

Consider, for example, the histogram represented in Figure
1. The class fractions are ranked in each case by educational
capital, and this ranking establishes (as you might expect)
reasonably neat correlations between educational capital and
musical preferences. If we rank the fractions by *economic*
capital, however — with 'secondary teachers', 'higher-educa-
tion teachers [and] art producers', and 'professions' slotted
after 'cultural intermediaries [and] art craftsmen', and with
'industrial and commercial employers' moved to the top of the
scale — the profiles look far less regular, as shown in Figure 2.
The sleight of hand by which the first histogram is
organized — the substitution of an educational for an
economic hierarchy — conceals the fact that, because of the
specialized relationship of the intelligentsia to culture, there
can be no immediate correlation of taste with class structure.[29]

[29] Similar difficulties beset Herbert Gans's attempt to correlate five 'taste
cultures' (high culture, upper-middle culture, lower-middle culture, low culture,
quasi-folk low culture) with social classes. The correlation falls down because

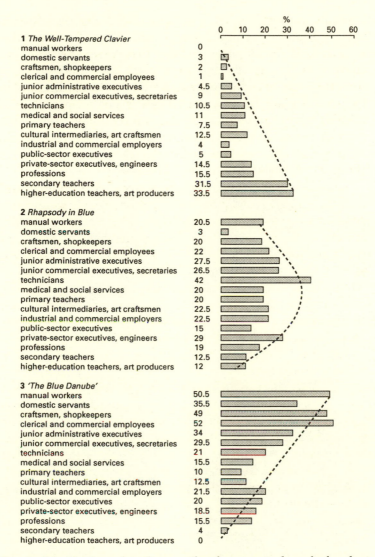

FIG. 1. *Distribution of preferences for three musical works by class fraction, ranked by educational capital*

Source: Bourdieu, *Distinction*, 17. Reprinted by permission of the publishers from *Distinction: A Social Critique of the Judgment of Taste*, by Pierre Bourdieu, Cambridge, Mass.: Harvard University Press, copyright © 1984 by the President and Fellows of Harvard College and Routledge and Kegan Paul Ltd.

FIG. 2. *Distribution of preferences of class fractions, ranked by economic capital*

Adapted from: Bourdieu, *Distinction*, 17 by permission of the publishers.

What Bourdieu does, in fact, is stress both the ideological incompatibility and the underlying class unity of the intelligentsia and the bourgeoisie. Thus he writes:

Through the mediation of the means of appropriation available to them, exclusively or principally cultural on the one hand, mainly economic on the other, and the different forms of relation to works of art which result from them, the different fractions of the dominant class are oriented towards cultural practices so different in their style and object and sometimes so antagonistic (those of 'artists' and 'bourgeois') that it is easy to forget that they are variants of the same fundamental relationship to necessity and to those who remain subject to it, and that each pursues the exclusive appropriation of legitimate cultural goods and the associated symbolic profits. (p. 176)

But again this is a sleight of hand, since the 'fundamental relationship to necessity' is structurally different in each case. On the one hand there is an investment of economic capital, a control over the means of production, and an extraction of surplus value from a workforce; on the other hand there is a position of wage labour or self-employment, a stock of cultural capital, and a delegated function of control. The conflation of these quite different positions in the relations of production indicates that something like an abstract concept of 'privilege' has been substituted for any more rigorous conception of class.

It is on the basis of the assumed unity of these two groups, however, that Bourdieu can then differentiate their systems of aesthetic preference. Whereas

the dominant fractions of the dominant class (the 'bourgeoisie') demand of art a high degree of denial of the social world and incline towards a hedonistic aesthetic of ease and facility, symbolized by boulevard theatre or Impressionist painting, the dominated fraction (the 'intellectuals' and 'artists') have affinities with the ascetic aspect of aesthetics and are inclined to support all artistic revolutions

high culture is linked to the intelligentsia (primarily academics and professionals), not to the upper class — and indeed Gans is unable to suggest any specific taste culture corresponding to this class. Herbert J. Gans, *Popular Culture and High Culture: An Analysis and Evaluation of Taste* (New York: Basic Books, 1974), esp. 71–81.

conducted in the name of purity and purification, refusal of ostentation and the bourgeois taste for ornament; and the dispositions towards the social world which they owe to their status as poor relations incline them to welcome a pessimistic representation of the social world.   (p. 176)

The more differentiated it becomes, the more this analysis comes to emphasize the antagonism 'between the life-styles corresponding to the opposing poles of the field of the dominant class' (p. 283). And the more this is the case, the more it undermines the postulate of a unitary 'dominant aesthetic' corresponding to a unitary 'aesthetic disposition'.

In the same way, Bourdieu's unification at the level of capital-equivalence of a 'dominant class' leads him to neglect the potential for contradiction in the role of the intelligentsia. The coincidence between the voting patterns of intellectuals and the working class seems to him 'paradoxical' (p. 438), and contradictions in political ideology are read as a sign of bad faith — in this passage, for example:

The members of the intellectual occupations (teachers, researchers, artists) declare themselves, more often than all other categories, 'supporters of revolutionary action', opposed to 'authoritarianism' and in favour of 'international class solidarity'. . . . But their answers often betray an ethos at variance with their discourse: they say more often than manual workers that their 'confidence in the trade unions' has declined since May 1968 or that an individual's most important characteristic is his personality (manual workers more often cite class) or that 'economic progress has benefited the majority' (workers more often think it has only benefited a minority). It may be that the tendency to political hyper-coherence which leads intellectuals to treat every problem as political and to seek perfect coherence in all attitudes in all areas of life is imposed on them by the fundamental discrepancy between their ethos and their discourse, especially when they originate from the dominated fractions of the dominant class.   (pp. 420–1)

The disparity between 'ethos' and 'discourse' is taken as an index of hypocrisy, and Bourdieu goes on to cite the 'nuances' of expression — evident only in the interview situation and too subtle to be reproduced in his text — which subvert the reality or the genuineness of these opinions. But the disparity could equally be read as a sign both of the possibility of contradiction within a class and within a class fraction (the intelligentsia has an unstable class location and is not itself unified), and of the power of cultural capital to motivate a partial break with the 'objective' determinants of class ethos and class condition. In Chapter 3 I shall elaborate a somewhat different account of the intelligentsia, emphasizing both its political ambivalence and the irreducibility of cultural capital to economic class.

The important point here is that, without a more complex analysis of the political and ideological functions of intellectuals, Bourdieu is unable to theorize relations of domination as relations of contested hegemony. Rather, he is forced to think in terms of a simple opposition between two discrete class and cultural formations. It is true that this rigid dichotomization is modified somewhat in later sections of the book: Bourdieu argues against the existence of an autonomous 'popular culture' and concludes that the urban working class 'remains fundamentally defined by the relation of dispossessed to possessor which links it to the bourgeoisie, in culture as in other areas' (p. 395); and he quotes Gramsci to support his argument that there are many features of the working-class lifestyle 'which, through the sense of incompetence, failure or cultural unworthiness, imply a form of recognition of the dominant values' (p. 386). But this dominance of the dominant values — which is never really given a historical and national specificity — then seems to become something absolute, and the working class to be inevitably and inexorably entrapped within the cultural limits imposed on it. Thus Bourdieu contends that 'the dominated, whose interests are bound up with the raising of consciousness, that is, with language, are at the mercy of the discourses that are presented to them; whenever they emerge from doxa they are liable to fall into allodoxia, into all the false recognitions encouraged by the dominant discourse' (p. 461); and even political insight is insufficient to break the hold of these false recognitions, since 'the most politically conscious fraction of the working class remains profoundly subject, in culture and language, to the dominant norms and values, and therefore deeply sensitive to the effects of authority imposition which every holder of cultural authority can exert' (p. 396). The totalizing grip of the 'dominant norms', understood as a unitary set of values, allows for no possibility of critique and social transformation.

Which makes it all the harder to understand what constitutes the possibility of Bourdieu's own critical exteriority to the dominant norms. Certainly it is not a *political* positioning which would inscribe its own class interest in the analysis, since Bourdieu detaches his categories from the political process. Nor is it given in the disrupted and ambivalent situation of the intelligentsia. One can only conclude that it is a purely philosophical, that is a purely *disciplinary*, authority that enables Bourdieu's work to stand outside and above the game of intellectual competition, outside the political imaginary, outside the categories of a dominant and all-embracing culture. Thus, writing of the specular dialectic of boulevard and avant-garde theatre, Bourdieu remarks that 'the whole process constitutes a perfect circle from which the only escape is to objectify it sociologically' (p. 235). It is the regime of truth ordering the discipline of *sociology* that yields the single point of exception to the 'labour of domination' (p. 511) performed by all (other) intellectual work,[30] and that allows Bourdieu to make the triumphal claim that his book has 'produced the truth of the taste against which, by an immense repression, the whole of legitimate aesthetics has been constructed' (p. 485). Written from an *impossible* perspective, a point that transcends the social space, Bourdieu's project ends up like the king in medieval social taxonomy, 'who, by setting himself up as the absolute subject of the classifying operation, as a principle external and superior to the classes it generated . . . assigned

---

[30] On this, see the exchange between Geng and Bourdieu in J.-M. Geng, *L'Illustre Inconnu* (Paris: Union Générale d'Éditions 10/18, 1978), 53–62, and Pierre Bourdieu, 'Sur l'objectivation participante', *Actes de la recherche en sciences sociales*, 23 (Sept. 1978), 67–9.

each group its place in the social order, and established himself as an unassailable vantage point' (p. 477).

The same thing cannot be said, or at least not in the same way, of the work of Michel de Certeau, since one of his main concerns in the analysis of the many disciplinary areas he has contributed to is with the ways in which disciplinary knowledges work to conceal the position and the interests of enunciation. In his writings on historiography, for example, he has paid particular attention to the way the historian's discourse 'gives itself credibility in the name of the reality which it is supposed to represent, but this authorized appearance of the "real" serves precisely to camouflage the practice which in fact determines it'.[31]

This is a crucial issue for the study of cultural economies, and I shall return to it later. For the moment, however, let me note that, in setting up the category of 'popular culture' as an object of analysis (particularly in *The Practice of Everyday Life*), Certeau operates a very interesting displacement which seeks to evade its essentialization as a distinct expressive domain. Rather than defining popular culture as a domain of texts or of artefacts, he understands it as a set of practices or operations performed on textual or text-like structures. His conception of operationality is deliberately very general, and this allows him to set up a series of criss-crossing metaphorical equivalences between different systems of practice (poaching, tricking, reading, speaking, strolling, shopping, desiring . . .), such that no single concept of 'doing' subsumes them all. They have in common, however, that they are *uses* of representations rather than representations in their own right. By means of this shift Certeau is able to move the analysis of popular culture away from the study of textuality, and in particular (while avoiding the psychologism of American 'uses and gratifications' analysis) to refuse

[31] Michel de Certeau, *Heterologies: Discourse on the Other*, trans. Brian Massumi, Theory and History of Literature, Vol. 17 (Minneapolis: University of Minnesota Press, 1986), 203; for a more extensive discussion see Michel de Certeau, *L'Écriture de l'histoire* (Paris: Gallimard, 1978).

the idea that textual effects are inherent in texts. On the contrary, indeed, 'the presence and circulation of a represen-tation . . . tells us nothing about what it is for its users. We must first analyse its manipulation by users who are not its makers.'[32] To use is not simply to apply, to put into practice, but to evade the prescriptions embedded in 'official' textuality. It opens up a gap between the two. Hence, as a general thesis, '*a way of using* imposed systems constitutes the resistance to the historical law of a state of affairs and its dogmatic legitimations . . . that is where the opacity of a "popular" culture could be said to manifest itself — a dark rock that resists all assimilation' (p. 18).

This appropriation of imposed systems involves users making 'innumerable and infinitesimal transformations of and within the dominant cultural economy in order to adapt it to their own interests and ends' (p. xiv). Transformation and adaptation can be thought of in terms of the metaphor of the manipulation of tools (a 'handling' that produces a bodily knowledge); or they can be thought of as a kind of production (a 'making' or '*poiesis*'). But as a making they are different from the 'official' system of production, hidden beneath its surface. This other system, or anti-system, could be called consumption, and indeed Certeau often refers to 'users' as consumers, and suggests a kind of privilege for the metaphor over all the others he employs (p. 33). But this is not consumption as inertia or as receptacle, opposed to the efficiency of its opposite principle; and Certeau refuses absolutely the valorization of 'authors, educators, revolution-aries, in a word, "producers", in contrast with those who do not produce' (p. 167). Rather, consumption is that set of tactics by which the weak make use of the strong. The polarity between consumption and production is dissolved, since

in reality, a rationalized, expansionist, centralized, spectacular and clamorous production is confronted by an entirely different kind of

---

[32] Michel de Certeau, *The Practice of Everyday Life*, trans. Steven Rendall (Berkeley: University of California Press, 1984), p. xiii. Further citations will be given in the text.

production, called 'consumption' and characterized by its ruses, its fragmentation (the result of the circumstances), its poaching, its clandestine nature, its tireless but quiet activity, in short by its quasi-invisibility, since it shows itself not in its own products (where would it place them?) but in an art of using those imposed on it.   (p. 31)

In its most literal sense consumption is an incorporation, a swallowing up of the external world; it is a *reduction* of cultural products to bodily matter. When Certeau wishes to stress the outgoing, creative, elaborative aspects of use he is more likely to use the metaphor of enunciation, in which the product of speech (the statement or *énoncé*) takes second place to the activity of producing it. Enunciation is governed by a small set of conditions: it is the realization, or the putting to use, of the language system; it involves a creative appropriation of this system; it depends upon an implicit contractual arrangement with the interlocutor; and it is governed by (but also reconstructs as a set of discursive co-ordinates) a particular organization of time and space (p. 33). It refers to linguistic practices, but can be extended to cover non-linguistic activities such as walking or cooking. And it is the basis for the construction of the rhetoric of ordinary conversation. This 'rhetoric', or repertoire of enunciative tactics,

consists of practices which transform 'speech situations', verbal productions in which the interlacing of speaking positions weaves an oral fabric without individual owners, creations of a communication that belongs to no one. Conversation is a provisional and collective effect of competence in the art of manipulating 'commonplaces' and the inevitability of events in such a way as to make them 'habitable'.   (p. xxii)

Rhetoric is the broader term by which Certeau designates the ruses, the jostling for position, the tropes and 'turns' that characterize all semiotic practice, and particularly the 'undignified' practices of the oppressed. Rhetoric is opposed, in Certeau's conceptual mapping, to the fantasy of linguistic propriety that governs scientific and technocratic reason; and to the myth of an impersonal and disinterested speech. What the turns of language lay bare is the fact that all speech is constructed in relation to an Other, and that it thus embodies a struggle for symbolic power. It is this that the rhetoric of everyday speech has in common with practical ruses:

in relation to the legalities of syntax and 'proper' sense, that is, in relation to the general definition of a 'proper' (as opposed to what is not 'proper'), the good and bad tricks of rhetoric are played on the terrain that has been set aside in this way. They are manipulations of language relative to occasions and are intended to seduce, captivate, or invert the linguistic position of the addressee. Whereas grammar watches over the 'propriety' of terms, rhetorical alterations (metaphorical drifts, elliptical condensations, metonymic miniaturizations, etc.) point to the use of language by speakers in particular situations of ritual or actual linguistic combat. (p. 39)

The practices of everyday life are coded by the same logic that informs the enunciative moves of rhetoric, but they do not conform to the laws of a coherent system (or anti-system). Rather, they are parasitic on the host system; they are 'multiform and fragmentary, relative to situations and details, insinuated into and concealed within devices whose mode of usage they constitute, and thus lacking their own ideologies and institutions' (p. xv). Thus, in talking about acts of appropriation of an urban system, Certeau speaks of 'microbe-like, singular and plural practices', a 'swarming activity' of procedures that have 'insinuated themselves into the networks of surveillance' (p. 96). The metaphorics is that of the infiltration of the body by micro-organisms, and their evasion both of the body's defence mechanisms and of the medical gaze. This invaded and manipulated body is no longer the organic body of the consumer but the body politic, the body of the State and of the bureaucratically calculated networks of the City.

The function of the City, with its rational articulation of space, is to administer and to control the practices of everyday life; but Certeau makes it clear that functions do not coincide with effects. The reference to surveillance (and, in the same passage, to 'panoptic administration') indicates that he wishes this argument to be read as a direct rejoinder to the Foucauldian concept of discipline. His quarrel is not with the concept itself, or with Foucault's account of its historical extension; rather, accepting the essentials of this account, he is concerned to discover and describe the ways in which populations manage to resist the encroachment of disciplinary mechanisms, the practices of evasive conformity by which they camouflage their 'miniscule' disruptions of an order they cannot openly contest. Certeau's task is thus the exact opposite of Foucault's: not

to make clear how the violence of order is transmuted into a disciplinary technology, but rather to bring to light the clandestine forms taken by the dispersed, tactical, and makeshift creativity of groups or individuals already caught in the nets of 'discipline'. Pushed to their ideal limits, these procedures and ruses of consumers compose the network of an antidiscipline.   (pp. xiv–xv)

The central metaphor here is the distinction between strategy and tactics, which Certeau superimposes on that between the large-scale manœuvring of a regular military unit and the tactical skirmishing of a guerrilla force. Strategy, he says, presupposes the separation of the 'subject of will and power' from its environment in order to make possible the imposition of this will. Strategy constructs places as fortifications, and thus as distinctly defined and possessed locations. Tactics, by contrast (the word at times has connotations of 'tact' — that is, the unspoken, intuitive practices of interpersonal relations), is a logic of momentary occupation without ownership. A set of procedures that 'produce without capitalizing' (without controlling time), it is 'articulated on situations and the will of others' (p. xx), its place 'belongs to the other. A tactic insinuates itself into the other's place, fragmentarily, without taking it over in its entirety, without being able to keep it at a distance' (p. xix).

The concept of place stands here for that exercise of self-control, of possession and self-possession, of propriety and security that, for Certeau, characterizes the structure of power. Where strategy seeks to occupy a terrain and to construct place according to an abstract model, tactics is 'a calculus which cannot count on a "proper" (a spatial or institutional localization), nor thus on a borderline distinguishing the other as a visible totality' (p. xix). The law it obeys is that of the *ligne d'erre*, the 'errant trajectory' that traverses space without occupying it or leaving a trace of its passage: a calculus of the random, then, and the unpredictable, since 'in the technocratically constructed, written, and functionalized space in which the consumers move about, their trajectories form unforeseeable sentences, partly unreadable paths across a space' (p. xviii).

Just as the initially stable category of production was reworked to take on the sense of the transformation of a system through consumption, however, so the categories of space and time, which are initially thought of as categories of power, undergo changes in the course of Certeau's exposition. The first move is to align strategy with space, and tactics with the use of time — and (since space and time are mutually dependent) this then entails an opposition between two different uses of time: 'strategies pin their hopes on the resistance that the *establishment of a place* offers to the erosion of time; tactics on a clever *utilization of time*, of the opportunities it presents and also of the play that it introduces into the foundations of power' (p. 34). The further move is then to demonstrate that space itself is riven by complexity. Although it seems to be depthless, a punctual disclosure of presence, space is in fact radically heterogenous, since 'the revolutions of history, economic mutations, demographic mixtures lie in layers within it, and remain there, hidden in customs, rites, and spatial practices' (p. 201). Apparently legible at a glance, it is in fact composed of overlaid fragments of language: the model here is Freud's description of the multiple archaeological layers of the city of Rome, which in turn acts as a model for the semiotic layering of the psyche. Concomitantly, the category of time loses its sense of calculability — or rather this sense is opposed to the concept of a contingent or 'casual' time which is 'narrated in the actual discourse of the city: an indeterminate fable, better articulated on the metaphorical practices and stratified places than on the empire of the evident in functionalist technocracy' (p. 203).

It is the possibility of *indeterminacy*, in the long run, that offers the best chance of popular resistance to technocratic rationality: not a resistance of one force or one reason to another, but an evasion of force and reason, an evasion of capture. The 'trajectories' of 'users' or 'consumers' are governed by the order of organized languages, spaces, and times, but they 'trace out the ruses of other interests and desires that are neither determined nor captured by the systems in which they develop' (p. xviii). Against the *conquiste* of the economy and the system of scripture, popular resistance mutely asserts the body and the materiality of the voice (p. 130).

Certeau gives two particularly powerful illustrations of the tactical reworking of a dominant system. The first is that of the subversive transformation by the conquered Indian peoples of South America of the 'successfully' imposed Spanish culture. While remaining submissive to their subjection, and even accepting of it, the Indian peoples 'often *made* of the rituals, representations, and laws imposed on them something quite different from what their conquerors had in mind; they subverted them not by rejecting or altering them, but by using them with respect to ends and references foreign to the system they had no choice but to accept'. This redirection of cultural structures involves the classic compromise of power-within-weakness: 'Their use of the dominant social order deflected its power, which they lacked the means to challenge; they escaped it without leaving it.' And Certeau makes the analogy directly with the uses made in contemporary societies 'by the "common people" of the culture disseminated and imposed by the "elites" producing the language' (p. xiii).

The other key illustration is that of '*la perruque*', 'the wig', which Certeau describes as 'the worker's own work disguised as work for his employer', and of which he writes:

Accused of stealing or turning material to his own ends and using the machines for his own profit, the worker who indulges in *la perruque* actually diverts time (not goods, since he uses only scraps) from the factory for work that is free, creative, and precisely not directed toward profit. In the very place where the machine he must serve reigns supreme, he cunningly takes pleasure in finding a way to create gratuitous products whose sole purpose is to signify his own capabilities through his *work* and to confirm his solidarity with other workers or his family through *spending* his time in this way. With the complicity of other workers (who thus defeat the competition the factory tries to instill among them), he succeeds in 'putting one over' on the established order on its home ground. Far from being a regression toward a mode of production organized around artisans or individuals, *la perruque* reintroduces 'popular' techniques of other times and other places into the industrial space (that is, into the Present order).   (pp. 25–6)

Rather than theft, then, *la perruque* is more akin to poaching, or to the creativity of a popular *poiesis*.

Both of these examples are models of transgression — models of that 'silent, transgressive, ironic or poetic activity of readers (or television viewers) who maintain their reserve in private and without the knowledge of the "masters"' (p. 173). The peculiar ambiguity of the problematic of transgression, however, lies in its total dependence upon the law that is to be transgressed. I can only transgress against the State or against God if I believe in them and in their authority; indeed, my very act of transgression confirms them in their authority, and confirms my need of them. This is exactly to 'escape without leaving'.[33] The same is more generally true of the relation to the other, the broad model (specified in various metaphors, such as that of host and parasite, or the occupation of

---

[33] Margaret Morse puts this into the historical perspective of a postmodern apparatus of representation when she writes that 'de Certeau's very means of escape are now designed into the geometries of everyday life, and his figurative practices of enunciation ("making do", "walking in the city", or "reading as poaching") are modeled in representation itself. Could de Certeau have imagined, as he wrote on walking as an evasive strategy of self-empowerment, that there would one day be video cassettes that demonstrate how to "power walk"?' Margaret Morse, 'An Ontology of Everyday Distraction: The Freeway, the Mall, and Television', in Patricia Mellencamp (ed.), *Logics of Television: Essays in Cultural Criticism* (Bloomington: Indiana University Press, 1990), 195.

someone else's terrain) through which Certeau theorizes popular resistance. By definition, the 'logic articulated on situations and the will of others' (p. xx) can never fundamentally challenge the order of power. It is integrated into the system it opposes, even as it undermines that system. The system understood as *game*, for example:

Innumerable ways of playing and foiling the other's game (*jouer/ déjouer le jeu de l'autre*), that is, the space instituted by others, characterize the subtle, stubborn, resistant activity of groups which, since they lack their own space, have to get along in a network of already established forces and representations. (p. 18)

To 'get along' is to be unable ever to challenge the ground rules themselves, ever to envisage the possibility of transforming the order of power. Certeau proposes a destabilization or a subversion of power, but only on condition that the hold of power is maintained. Despite his criticism of the totalizing force of Foucault's conception of discipline, his own vision of domination is monolithic: power is held absolutely or not held at all.

The first of the arguments I want to make against Certeau, then, concerns his understanding of power. Nowhere in his work is there anything other than a polar model of domination, according to which sovereign power is exercised by a ruling class (or, more often, by an 'élite'; or else by a technocracy or a technocratic rationality defined without reference to class) over a mass of oppressed popular subjects who lack all power. It is true that these subject groups exercise an art of the weak which modifies or deflects the power of the dominant order, but the flow of power is nevertheless all in the one direction and from a singular source. Rather than being defined by complexity, diversity, and ambiguity, the struggle for social power is ultimately thought in terms of a simple pathos of resistance.

One reason for this is perhaps that Certeau's privileged examples of popular resistance are drawn from peasant cultures; and, more importantly, that the class-specificity of political struggle is lost in the figure of 'le pleb', 'ordinary people': a figure that eternalizes popular struggle as a continuous tradition extending from tribal cultures through to an undifferentiated contemporary urban populace. There is no room here for the complexities and confusions of hegemonic struggle; for struggles and rivalries *between* the groups comprising 'the people'; or for complicity in and acceptance of domination (the current wave of Christian fundamentalism in Latin America, for example, which is inspired and financed by American evangelists and directly serves American interests in the continent, is a forceful example of the identification of the dominated with the values of a hegemonic group, and one that partly contradicts Certeau's argument about the reworking by indigenous peoples of an earlier wave of imperialist culture).[34] These problems are inherent, I think, in the conception of 'the people' as a unified bloc, the composition of which transcends class differences; and in the assumption that this bloc necessarily operates in a progressive way. I shall return to these questions in the next chapter when I consider in more depth the problem of the politics of populism.

The second argument that I want to make against Certeau concerns the problem of the textual form in which we have access to the 'doings' of popular culture. In order to broach this question I want to consider one final metaphor of these doings, that of reading.

Reading, it should go without saying, is understood in Certeau's writings not as a passive absorption of information,

---

[34] The problem is that of the extent to which it is possible to generalize from particular historical examples. In a somewhat different context, Nicholas Thomas has written of the importance of recognizing 'that material products, as well as belief systems such as Christianity, or resources such as literacy, are always acted upon and reformulated by indigenous populations, but these acts of derivation and displacement take place as political circumstances change, and the real ramifications of the entanglement of local polities in wider relations need to be appreciated'. Nicholas Thomas, *Entangled Objects: Exchange, Material Culture, and Colonialism in the Pacific* (Cambridge, Mass.: Harvard University Press, 1991), 186. Nothing, that is to say, guarantees that the uses made of a dominant culture will be subversive ones.

an effect of the book,[35] but as a creative processing, 'a silent production: the drift across the page, the metamorphosis of the text effected by the wandering eyes of the reader, the improvisation and expectation of meanings inferred from a few words, leaps over written spaces in an ephemeral dance' (p. xxi). Reading is poaching, ruse, metaphor, invention, self-pluralization, adaptation, insinuation (pp. xxi–xxii). It is singular and unorganized, the opposite of a systemic activity, since 'to read is to wander through an imposed system' (p. 169). And it is potentially a political activity, since it is the basis for a broader transformation of the social relationships that overdetermine the reader's relation to texts (p. 173).

At the same time, research into reading is rendered difficult by 'the lack of traces left behind by a practice that slips through all sorts of "writings"' (p. 170). Like walking, which is transient and fully subject to time, reading produces no storage of information; it is pure process, without textual form. And this is surely more generally true of the various operations that Certeau subsumes under the concept of 'doing': poaching, tricking, speaking, walking, all lack textual realization.

This is not the whole story, however. As soon as we ask whether these doings, these *arts de faire*, are merely contingent — pure, unstructured actions, detached from any semiotic co-ordinates — it becomes apparent that there is another dimension to Certeau's thinking. In this more structural aspect of his analysis he makes it clear that he is in fact concerned with 'modes of operation or schemata of action' rather than with actions in themselves, or with the subjects of these actions. To be more precise, operations are rule-governed, and we can therefore distinguish between practices and an underlying 'ensemble of *procedures*' which are 'schemas of operations and of technical manipulations' (p.

---

[35] Michel de Certeau, 'La Lecture absolue (Théorie et pratique des mystiques chrétiens: XVIe–XVIIe siècles)', in Lucien Dällenbach and Jean Ricardou (eds.), *Problèmes actuels de la lecture*, Colloques de Cérisy (Paris: Clancier-Guénaud, 1982), 67.

43). In relation to the 'official' systems governing the organization of social life, these disruptive 'styles' of operating are equally *systemic*; they are 'systems of operational combination [*combinatoires d'opération*]' (p. xi), and the relevant model for describing them would therefore not be that of the opposition of a systemic *langue* to an unstructured *parole* but rather that of the relation between *langue* and the system of discourse.[36] It is in this sense that Certeau writes that the schemata of action

intervene in a field which regulates them at a first level (for example, at the level of the factory system), but they introduce into it a way of turning it to their advantage that obeys other rules and constitutes something like a second level interwoven into the first (for instance, *la perruque*). These 'ways of operating' are similar to 'instructions for use', and they create a certain play in the machine through a stratification of different and interfering kinds of functioning.   (p. 30)

Finally, and again resembling the codes that govern the production of discourse, the codes of practice are situation-specific; any act implies 'a logic of the operation of actions relative to types of situations' (p. 21).

I emphasize the semiotic and systemic dimension of Certeau's categories in part because it is easy to miss it in his insistence on the singularity and particularity of practices, but also in order to indicate that he is concerned with elaborating something like an ethnography of actions through an analysis of the codes of practice that constitute a culture. These codes are, in one sense, *like texts*, and there is thus a certain circularity in the move — initially enlightening as I think it is — from texts to uses of texts. The point is that uses and doings are codified, and that these generative codes will necessarily feed back into the process of textual production. There are no codes of reading to which there will not correspond (at least potentially) a set of codes of writing. The appeal to a pristine (and invisible) *experience* of the text is both unwarranted and in principle dangerous.

[36] Cf. Michel Pêcheux, *Les Vérités de la Palice* (Paris: Maspéro, 1975).

The danger is this: that in the absence of realized texts which can be subjected to determinate analysis — in the absence of a definite and graspable object — the analyst will inevitably reconstruct such an object. This will usually be done either through a direct substitution of the analyst's own experience (whether or not it is acknowledged as such) for that of the user, or through indirect modes of textual objectification, such as the administration of question-naires.[37] In both cases there is a politically fraught substitution of the voice of a middle-class intellectual for that of the subject of popular or indigenous culture; and it is character-istically in the space of this substitution that the categories of the popular and the indigenous are constructed.

---

[37] David Morley's analysis of the responses of diverse groups to a television programme, for example, makes the mistake of confusing responses given in interview with the direct experience of the programme; the mediating sociological apparatus is simply disregarded (David Morley, The 'Nationwide' Audience: Structure and Decoding. London: BFI, 1980). Morley has admonished me for a previous version of this criticism in which I mistakenly spoke of his use of 'texts written in the conventional genre of the questionnaire answer'; with this factual correction, however, I believe that the methodological criticism still stands (cf. David Morley, Television Audiences and Cultural Studies (London: Routledge, 1992), 10–11). A similar criticism can be made of Janice Radway's 'ethnographic' practices in Reading the Romance: Women, Patriarchy, and Popular Literature (Chapel Hill: University of North Carolina Press, 1984).

2

The Concept of the Popular

> The history of the many deceptions which have been
> practised with this concept of the people is a long and
> complicated one—a history of class struggles.[1]

A substitution of voices: this is a question, then, of
representation, in the political sense of speaking, or claiming
to speak, on behalf of someone else. But it is equally a
question of the representation of a theoretical object, the
system of relations of cultural value as it works to organize
the play of self and other. The models developed by Bourdieu
and Certeau both, for all their cogency, generate major
problems in the theorization of relations of cultural value.
Both tend to fix an essential domain of the popular, without
ever specifying its institutional characteristics; both work with
a top-down model of social domination; and both tend to
slight the complexities of the relation of the class (or class
fraction) of intellectuals to 'high' culture and to 'popular'
culture.

The inadequacy of an affirmative conception of popular
culture becomes particularly salient when it is translated into
the disciplinary structures of cultural studies. Let me take as
one influential example that can stand for many the work of
John Fiske. For Fiske, the category of popular culture in
advanced capitalist societies is defined not by its industrial
mode of production but by the extent to which cultural
products are able to 'bear the interests of the people'.[2] There is

---

[1] Bertolt Brecht, 'Against Georg Lukács', trans. Stuart Hood, *Aesthetics and Politics* (London: New Left Books, 1977), 81.

[2] John Fiske, *Understanding Popular Culture* (Boston: Unwin Hyman, 1989), 23. Further citations will be given in the text.

a strict separation between the industrial and cultural economies, between commodities and the uses made of them: 'At the point of sale the commodity exhausts its role in the distribution economy, but begins its work in the cultural. Detached from the strategies of capitalism, its work for the bosses completed, it becomes a resource for the culture of everyday life' (p. 35).

The point of splitting the function of cultural products into two distinct stages is to free the process of circulation and reception of the text from any contamination or limitation by its industrial origins. It is a way of at once asserting and denying the relevance of the conditions of production to the workings of the text.[3] On the basis of this strategic separation Fiske can then perform a further act of purification, this time by protecting popular readings from any contamination by hegemonic values. This involves endowing the popular with a political essence: 'There can be no popular dominant culture, for popular culture is formed always in reaction to, and never as part of, the forces of domination' (p. 43). Any non-oppositional reading of a text (for example, a reading of *Dallas* that accepts its 'capitalist, consumerist, sexist, racist values') (p. 44) is *therefore* not a popular reading. 'The people', that is to say, by definition subscribe to none of these values; incorrect values come only from the ruling class. In the same way, Fiske will concede that there are certain pleasures to be had from identifying with the order of power. 'The pleasures of conformity by which power and its disciplinary thrust are internalized are real pleasures and are widely experienced. They are not, however, popular pleasures, but hegemonic ones' (p. 49). The popular is thus sanitized by the expulsion from it of all ambivalence, all complexity, all

[3] Simon Frith argues that this has been a standard strategy in cultural studies since Adorno: 'The analytic move . . . has been to accept the Frankfurt reading of cultural production and to look for the redeeming features of commodity culture in the act of consumption. . . . In British subcultural theory, this reworking took on the particular form of identifying certain social groups with what we might call "positive mass consumption" . . . The value of cultural goods could therefore be equated with the value of the groups consuming them—youth, the working class, women, and so forth.' Frith, 'The Good, the Bad, and the Indifferent', 103.

perverse pleasure, and it becomes clear that the category is purely prescriptive (that is to say, a fantasy). 'Hegemonic force can be exercised only if the people choose to read the texts that embody it, and they will choose only those texts that offer opportunities to resist, evade, or scandalize it' (p. 105). Why will they? Because they are defined as those who will do so. If they do not, then by definition they are not (acting as) 'the people'.

'Effective power is homogeneous':[4] the model of power at work here, as (with somewhat more complexity) in Certeau, is one that opposes repression to resistance, the 'imperializing' to the 'localizing'; although it is at times called a Foucauldian conception of power,[5] it is in fact the model that Foucault calls the juridico-discursive, and it is structured around a set of binary antagonisms: 'strategies opposed by tactics, the bourgeoisie by the proletariat; hegemony met by resistance, ideology countered or evaded; top-down power opposed by bottom-up power, social discipline faced with disorder' (p. 47). Good opposes evil: this is essentially an ethical under-standing of power, and it has the antithetical structure of a moralized politics. The figure has two consequences: the first is that the popular is understood as a homogeneous will, and all its expressions are by definition politically virtuous. The second is that cultural variation comes to bear an immediate political significance. Thus the wearing of torn jeans, or listening to rock music, or going shopping all work as models of political resistance and opposition to 'the power-bloc'.[6]

---

[4] John Fiske, *Power Plays, Power Works* (London: Verso, 1993), 204.

[5] Ibid. 11.

[6] By contrast, Connor writes of the rock music industry as 'probably the best example of the process by which contemporary capitalist culture promotes or multiplies difference in the interests of maintaining its profit structure. If there is a dominant in contemporary rock music, it is the dominance of multiple marginality. In this sense, Hebdige, Lipsitz and McRobbie are right to celebrate marginal rock music as representatively postmodern, but wrong to assume that its energies are necessarily in a liberalizing direction. Far from decentring or undermining the structures of the rock industry, each eruption of cultural difference only serves to stabilize this culture, by spreading and diversifying its boundaries.' Steven Connor, *Postmodernist Culture: An Introduction to Theories of the Contemporary* (Oxford: Basil Blackwell, 1989), 189–90.

Any purely bodily pleasure, such as that given by hard drugs or loud rock music, is a priori subversive, since it breaks down the socially constructed self (p. 50). And to watch television is to make 'scandalous, oppositional meanings' (p. 36). It is a politics without effects (summed up, perhaps, in the *psychological* orientation of the category of 'empowerment') which offers little disturbance to the real social relations of advanced capitalism.[7]

The step from analysis of texts to analysis of the workings of texts is not, in principle, a wrong one. It could, in principle, have produced something like a *Wirkungsgeschichte* of mass-cultural texts (a history of the work done *by* but also *upon* them), which would pay careful attention to the structured regimes of reading governing textual interpretation and adaptation. The problem lies in the positing of texts and readers as separate, atomized entities, and in the essentialization of a 'popular' regime of reading as having intrinsic and unchanging characteristics. As it happens, Fiske is unwilling to abandon textual determinacy altogether, and develops the concept of the 'producerly' text to account for the fact that it is not just any texts (for example, it is not 'high'-cultural texts) that become 'popular'; texts are 'discursively limited or bounded',[8] and thus 'offer' a relevance that is then taken up by the *reader's* criteria of relevance. In one sense this means that the work of resistance is always already embedded in the text itself; the producerly text, like the text of deconstruction, is the one that 'exposes, however reluctantly, the vulnerabilities, limitations, and weaknesses of its own preferred meanings' (p. 104). At the same time, Fiske is unwilling to grant the text any power to govern its reading. Rather, 'the viewer makes meanings and pleasures from [the text] that are

[7] Tim Rowse, 'Reply to John Fiske's Paper', *Continuum*, 1: 2 (1988), 68–9, questions whether the meanings generated by subordinate groups are oppositional to or merely different from those of the dominant culture, and sets out the presuppositions necessary for this to be the case. These are, primarily, that there be a dominant interest in the imposition of a monolithic set of cultural values—which Rowse argues is not true of most advanced capitalist societies.

[8] John Fiske, 'Critical Response: Meaningful Moments', *Critical Studies in Mass Communication* (Sept. 1988), 248.

relevant to his or her social allegiances at the moment of viewing; the criteria for relevance *precede* the viewing moment'.[9] Texts are 'passive',[10] no more than an effect of perceived relevance. We thus return to a very traditional theory of communication, in which persons are external to the process of textual signification rather than being intricated, in a process of repetitive constitution, with the play of meaning.

In this schema the formation of the subject takes place prior to and separate from the encounter with the text, in a space of social allegiances that is therefore deemed to be pre-textual. The methodological problem here, as always, is the double one of how I can know what constitutes relevance or value for someone else when I don't necessarily have any textual traces to work on; and how I can speak of the values of the other from a position of difference both in culture and in status. Fiske solves this dual problem by simply collapsing the differences between the subject and the object of analysis. The form this takes is, on the one hand, the adoption of a first-person voice which claims identification with the 'vulgar tastes and democratic inclinations' (p. 59) of popular culture—against the grain of the analyst's objective class-affiliation; and, on the other, the use of an ethnographic (or indeed 'autoethnographic')[11] approach which

allows subordinate groups some say in explaining and under-standing their own social position and their own cultural processes.

[9] John Fiske, 'Critical Response: Meaningful Moments', 247.
[10] Ibid. 248.
[11] John Fiske, 'Ethnosemiotics: Some Personal and Theoretical Reflections', *Cultural Studies*, 4: 1 (Jan. 1990), 90. For a critique, cf. Virginia Nightingale, 'What's "Ethnographic" about Ethnographic Audience Research?', *Australian Journal of Communication*, 16 (1989), 50–63. Nightingale lists a number of inadequacies with the use of so-called ethnographic methods in cultural studies, including 'the apparently absolute refusal to apply principles of "readership", particularly those which stress the recognition that meaning is as much in the reader as in the text, to the reading of research "texts" such as interviews, letters, diaries etc., as read by the researcher' (p. 53); and she concludes that 'what occurs . . . in the absence of rigorous ethnographic observation and description, when the techniques of ethnography are divorced from ethnographic process, is a co-opting of the interviewee's experience of the text by the researcher, and its use as authority for the researcher's point of view' (p. 55).

There is also a deliberate, though still undeveloped, attempt by some of these [cultural] workers to position themselves as fans alongside those they are studying and thus to avoid the danger of speaking for them.[12]

It should be clear that I am deeply suspicious of this claim that 'the people' can speak *through* the position of the analyst, or, conversely, that the class position of a middle-class intellectual can be put to one side when one writes 'as a fan'. As Jostein Gripsrud argues, the claim both erases the socio-cultural differences between intellectuals and the core audiences of popular genres, and disregards the specificity of the reading practices of intellectuals, which are based on competence in a variety of cultural codes: 'Our ability to take part in both high and low culture's codes and practices is a class privilege; it does not mean that the socially operative distinction between the two spheres has ceased to exist.'[13]

> The Bororos of Brazil sink slowly into their collective death, and Lévi-Strauss takes his seat in the French Academy.[14]

Paradoxically, it is in Certeau's work that we can find the sharpest questioning of the complicity with domination involved in the study or indeed the espousal of a 'popular' whose distance and difference are suppressed. 'How', he asks, 'is it possible to foil here and now the social hierarchization which organizes scientific work on popular culture and repeats itself in that work?' (p. 130). One answer, tentatively offered, is that the tactical procedures of *la perruque* can serve as the model, within academic writing, of an unorthodox analysis capable of studying the popular without constructing an authoritative metadiscourse (pp. 25, 28). But this model is never satisfactorily explored, and Certeau's counter-argument,

---

[12] Fiske, 'Critical Response', 250.

[13] Jostein Gripsrud, '"High Culture" Revisited', *Cultural Studies*, 3: 2 (May 1989), 204.

[14] Michel de Certeau, *The Practice of Everyday Life*, trans. Steven Rendall (Berkeley: University of California Press, 1984), 25.

that the study of popular culture has historically always gone hand in hand with its suppression or co-optation,[15] is a good deal more convincing. His key example, described in meticulous detail in *Une politique de la langue*,[16] is that of the first analyses of French *patois*. These investigations, conducted under the supervision of the Abbé Grégoire, have as their aim simultaneously to collect and describe a vast corpus of linguistic materials, and to recommend the destruction of the regional *patois* in favour of a universalization of 'the French language'. 'The ethnologist and the archaeologist arrive at the moment a culture has lost its means of self-defence',[17] and the search for the authenticity of a subordinate culture is grounded in a masking of the analyst's own political interest—an interest in 'the elimination of a popular menace'.[18]

It is this exemplary suspicion of Certeau's that is lacking in so many accounts of the popular in contemporary cultural studies. Let me briefly mention another version of this ethnography of the popular, that of Iain Chambers. Like Certeau, Chambers operates with the model of an active process of consumption of cultural goods in which 'style'

[15] Michel de Certeau, *Heterologies: Discourse on the Other*, trans. Brian Massumi, Theory and History of Literature, Vol. 17 (Minneapolis: University of Minnesota Press, 1986), 119.

[16] Michel de Certeau, Dominique Julia, and Jacques Revel, *Une politique de la langue: La Révolution française et les patois: L'enquête de Grégoire* (Paris: Gallimard, 1975), esp. 160–9.

[17] Certeau, *Heterologies*, 123.

[18] Ibid. 128. Peter Burke, 'The "Discovery" of Popular Culture', in Raphael Samuel (ed.), *People's History and Socialist Theory* (London: Routledge, 1981), 216–26, makes a similar argument that the intellectuals who, following the pioneering work of Herder and the brothers Grimm, 'discovered' popular culture, came predominantly from the upper classes, 'to whom the people were a mysterious "other", described in terms of everything these discoverers were not (or thought they were not; natural, simple, instinctive, irrational, and rooted in the local soil)' (p. 216). And Susan Stewart, writing about the ballad 'scandals' of eighteenth-century England, draws the same conclusion as Certeau about the effect of the 'discovery' of popular forms: 'The *writing* of oral genres always results in a residue of lost context and lost presence that literary culture . . . imbues with a sense of nostalgia and even regret. We might consider the writing of folklore in this sense to be, then, a method for making oral genres extinct.' Susan Stewart, *Crimes of Writing: Problems in the Containment of Representation* (New York: Oxford University Press, 1991), 104.

becomes a transformative force. Within the subculture of the mods, for example,

consumerism was turned into the secret language of style, into imposing your presence on the goods, on the present. The mod subculture proceeded to demonstrate how the objects and contexts of commercial popular culture—records, clothes, dance, transport, drugs—could be transformed and moulded by the particular realities of *this* time and *this* place.[19]

Members of the subculture 'rendered consumption into a precise and imaginative conquest of their circumstances' (p. 7).

One might question whether the subculture was 'moulding' the commodities or functioned rather as a vehicle for commodity circulation. But what I am concerned with here is the aesthetic dichotomy within which this image of the subculture is formed. The opposition is between 'the official universe of culture', identified with the 'old continent', and popular culture, identified with a range of American values.[20] This historically specific relationship is then solidified into a more universal dichotomy between two cultural orders:

Official culture, preserved in art galleries, museums, and university courses, demands cultivated tastes and a formally imparted knowledge. It demands moments of attention that are separated from the run of daily life. Popular culture, meanwhile, mobilizes the tactile, the incidental, the transitory, the expendable; the visceral. It does not involve an abstract aesthetic research amongst privileged objects of attention, but invokes mobile orders of sense, taste and desire. (p. 12)[21]

---

[19] Iain Chambers, *Popular Culture: The Metropolitan Experience* (London: Methuen, 1986), 7. Further references will be given in the text.

[20] On the force of American stylistic values—for example, that of 'streamlining'—on other cultures in the 1950s and 1960s, cf. Dick Hebdige, *Hiding in the Light: On Images and Things* (London and New York: Routledge/Comedia, 1988), esp. 45–76. More generally on American Fordist design, cf. Terry Smith, *Making the Modern: Industry, Art, and Design in America* (Chicago: University of Chicago Press, 1993).

[21] There is a similarly tendentious construction of the relations between popular and 'official' culture in Ken Worpole's *Reading By Numbers*. Having initially established the stranglehold of highly standardized and rationalized

One problem with this thesis is that, in setting up spontaneous pleasure against formal learning, it plays down the part of learning and discrimination in all cultural formation (think, for example, of the effort that teenagers put into constructing a learned canon of recorded music, and of the whole pop-scholarly apparatus that goes into that construction).[22] But the more serious consequence of this dichotomy occurs when it is extrapolated into an epistemo-logical opposition between, on the one hand, the 'cerebral world of official culture', the 'contemplative stare', based in 'the authority of the academic mind that seeks to explain an experience that is rarely personal' and is characterized by its 'rarity'; and, on the other, a 'popular epistemology' which is 'an informal knowledge of the everyday based on the sensory, the immediate, the pleasurable and the concrete' (p. 13).

commercial publishing and distribution over book production in the UK—to the exclusion of 'alternative' forms of writing by working-class people, ethnic groups, feminists, gays, and lesbians—Worpole then quite unaccountably sets out to hold 'the Oxbridge literary world-view' responsible for the choking-off of popular cultural forms which he now identifies with the market-place. Ken Worpole, *Reading By Numbers: Contemporary Publishing and Popular Fiction* (London: Comedia, 1984), 5, 12–13. Parallel contradictions are to be found in John Docker's defence of mass-cultural forms as an 'expression of authentic working-class values' (John Docker, 'In Defence of Popular Culture', *Arena*, 60 (1982), 82), which then leads him to a simple valorization of the commercial media over the 'elitist' state-owned media: a position that puts him squarely in the same camp as Rupert Murdoch, himself (when occasion suits) a convinced defender of popular taste. Cf. also John Docker, 'Give Them Facts—the Modern Gradgrinds', *Media Information Australia*, 30 (Nov. 1983), 3–7; Ingrid Hagstrom, 'Popular Culture Undefined', *Arena*, 61 (1982), 141–8; Anthony Ashbolt, 'Against Left Optimism: A Reply to John Docker', *Arena*, 61 (1982), 132–40; Keith Windschuttle, *The Media* (Ringwood: Penguin, 1984); William Routh, 'Keith Windschuttle's Media', *Australian Journal of Cultural Studies*, 3: 1 (1985), 128–34.

[22] Simon Frith writes that young people's involvement in rock music 'rests on a substantial body of knowledge and an active sense of choice—musicians and audiences alike have a clear understanding of genre rules and histories, can hear and place sounds in terms of influence and source, have no hesitation about making and justifying judgements of musical meaning and value', and have a 'positively Adornoesque contempt' for commercial formulae. Thus 'the pedagogical difference between rock and classical music . . . is not that one group is taught, one untaught, but that they are taught differently, in different institutions, though often according to the same values'. Simon Frith, 'The Cultural Study of Popular Music', in *Cultural Studies*, ed. Lawrence Grossberg, Cary Nelson, and Paula Treichler (New York: Routledge, 1992), 174–5.

It is not so much for what it says about popular ways of knowing that the dichotomy is theoretically dubious, as for the way Chambers—in a gesture that Andrew Ross calls 'a kind of elaborate blackface'[23]—seeks to appropriate this streetwise epistemology for his own academic discourse. This is a knowledge that, when put to use in a book *about* popular culture, denies its own expository and analytic—its *intellectual*—status, and indeed positively masks it in the anti-intellectual opposition of the 'visceral' to the 'cerebral' (p. 13). If I wish to question, for example, why it is that the history recounted in Chambers's Introduction has this particular form—why it begins with the Stones rather than with Elvis or with music-hall—or indeed to ask what it's a history *of*, I can only be referred to the series of images that 'do not so much "verify" what I have to say as refer back to themselves' (pp. 12–13): which is precisely what I want to question. It's an epistemology that can never be wrong because it can never be contested. And it constructs a politics of the popular in which 'the people' is not simply the object of study but is also 'the textually delegated, allegorical emblem of the critic's own activity. Their *ethnos* may be constructed as other, but it is used as the ethnographer's mask.'[24]

All theoretical accounts of contemporary popular culture are caught within a tension that seems to be constitutive of the concept.

On the one hand there is a widespread and historically hard-learned perception of the need to recognize the specificity of textual transactions. This entails theorizing the readers or spectators of texts as actively engaging with and constructing textual meaning (and themselves as subjects in the process), and it means refusing the argument that texts impose meaning, that they unilaterally shape the consciousness or the political opinions of their readers. Texts become a

[23] Ross, *No Respect*, 6.
[24] Meaghan Morris, 'Banality in Cultural Studies', *Discourse*, X: 2 (Spring–Summer 1988), 17.

locus of struggle in which the business of belief is negotiated by readers choosing textual sense on the basis of their worldly experience.

On the other hand, it remains important to define the systemic constraints within which textual choice is possible. Contemporary mass media texts are an integral part of a system of commodity production, in several ways: they are themselves commodities, produced within serial processes according to industrial formulae based on intensive market research; in the case of the commercially funded parts of the print and electronic media, they have the function of delivering audiences as commodities to advertisers (so that, paradoxically, advertisements must be seen not as contingent interruptions to a primary flow of text but as themselves the nodal points of this flow); and they are directly bound up, through the gratifications they offer or allude to, with the sale of commodities and of capitalist culture as a whole.

There is no simple way (apart from straightforward reductionism) of squaring a methodological concentration on the productive working of texts with a methodological concentration on the productive work of the system. They are not complementary, and the effect of this tension is a kind of necessary indeterminacy principle. Both positions are 'correct', but there is no way of reconciling them in a single perspective. By the same token, to elaborate a 'correct' position is therefore by definition to fail to perform the countervailing analysis.

The major stakes in the interpretation of cultural relations are thus those of an impossible synthesis, and the major theoretical impulses have been those which attempt to deal with the paradox of mutually incompatible arguments which are not amenable to adjustment within a totalizing framework (the 'systemic' account is itself already totalizing), or within a dialectic of the general and the particular, of the global and the local.

One of the most important attempts to negotiate a theoretical middle ground, that of Stuart Hall and others at the Centre for Contemporary Cultural Studies, derives its force from the Gramscian concept of hegemony, and particularly from the thesis that, rather than being imposed from above, the power of the dominant class, if it is to be capable of legitimacy and self-reproduction, must in some sense be acceptable to the dominated classes; power must be 'popular'. From this follows a careful definition of the inherent ambivalence of popular cultural forms.

Thus, in an exemplary essay, Hall writes of 'the double-stake in popular culture, the double movement of containment and resistance, which is always inevitably inside it'.[25] 'Inside' is not quite the right metaphor, however, since popular culture is not a definite configuration of texts or practices. It is neither the particular set of popular traditions of resistance to social and cultural transformations, nor the forms which structure these traditions: it is something more abstract, 'the ground on which the transformations are worked' (p. 28), and the particular figures that organize the popular at any one time can only properly be studied in relation to the conditions of possibility that constitute this ground.

In order to get at the sense in which 'the popular' is different from any particular content and from any singular expression of power or resistance, Hall broaches three successive definitions. The first, a quantitative or 'market' definition corresponding to a capitalist 'common sense', says simply that certain things 'are said to be "popular" because masses of people listen to them, buy them, read them, consume them, and seem to enjoy them' (p. 231). Popular culture in this sense is in conflict with a qualitatively defined 'culture of the people', a culture understood as emanating *from* the people, and it is associated with the manipulation and debasement of this culture. Nevertheless, it would be quite wrong to see the consumers of commercially produced culture as passive dupes (this is 'a deeply unsocialist perspective') (p. 232), and the theoretical problem thus posed is that of avoiding such a condemnation whilst remaining

---

[25] Stuart Hall, 'Notes on Deconstructing "the Popular"', in Raphael Samuel (ed.), *People's History and Socialist Theory* (London: Routledge, 1981), 228.

attentive to the ideological functions of commercial popular culture.

This is close to Tony Bennett's stress on the political importance of addressing 'the people' 'in the actual forms of their cultural constitution in advanced capitalism',[26] and it means that it is not a valid solution to counterpose a debased commercial culture to an 'authentic' popular culture. Culture can only be thought in terms of relations *between* classes, and Hall therefore asserts that 'there is *no* whole, authentic, autonomous "popular culture" which lies outside the field of force of the relations of cultural power and domination' (p. 232). The cultural can be thought neither as expressive freedom nor as externally imposed constraint. It is precisely because popular culture is located on, or indeed *is*, a contested ground, however, that it must be understood in terms of struggle over how the world is to be understood—a struggle over the terms of our experience of the world. And the struggle is of importance only because it is really capable of *forming* popular experience:

If the forms of provided commercial popular culture are not purely manipulative, then it is because, alongside the false appeals, the foreshortenings, the trivializations and shortcircuits, there are also elements of recognition and identification, something approaching a recreation of recognisable experiences and attitudes to which people are responding.   (p. 233)

There are traces of an unreconstructed mimeticism here, but the emphasis on the structure of contradictory value that characterizes popular culture has the strategic value of moving away from essentialist definitions of the popular.

From here, Hall passes to a second, 'descriptive' definition of the popular, according to which 'popular culture is all those things that "the people" do or have done' (p. 234). This definition provides an infinitely expanding inventory, but it is only meaningful in so far as it can contain this expansion by opposing the popular to whatever counts as the non-popular.

[26] Tony Bennett, 'Marxist Cultural Politics: In Search of "the Popular"', *Australian Journal of Cultural Studies*, 1: 2 (1983), 21.

This opposition cannot be set up in a purely descriptive way, however, for it takes different forms in different historical periods. A *general* account of the popular can thus not be achieved in terms of constant class categories, because the content of each category changes historically. Instead, the interdependent terms popular/non-popular must be thought as a structural principle, sustained by particular institutional configurations at any one time.

On this basis Hall is then able to propose a third (if 'uneasy') definition which insists that 'what is essential to the definition of popular culture is the relations which define "popular culture" in a continuing tension (relationship, influence and antagonism) to the dominant culture'. Two consequences flow from this. The first is an argument that aesthetic forms have no inherent meaning or value. Most cultural forms are

composed of antagonistic and unstable elements. The meaning of a cultural form and its place or position in the cultural field is *not* inscribed inside its form. Nor is its position fixed once and forever. . . . The meaning of a cultural symbol is given in part by the social field into which it is incorporated, the practices with which it articulates and is made to resonate.   (p. 235)

There can therefore be no fixed inventory of forms (describing the novel, for example, as a 'bourgeois' form, as though it could never be anything else), nor can there be a 'universal popular aesthetic, founded on the moment of origin of cultural forms and practices' (p. 237).

The second consequence is that 'there is no one-to-one relationship between a class and a particular cultural form or practice', because

there are no wholly separate 'cultures' paradigmatically attached, in a relation of historical fixity, to specific 'whole' classes—although there are clearly distinct and variable class-cultural formations. Class cultures tend to intersect and overlap in the same field of struggle. The term 'popular' indicates this somewhat displaced relationship of culture to classes.   (p. 238)

Taken together these theses—familiar and even orthodox as they may now sound—seem to me adequately to counter the essentializing constructions of Bourdieu and, to a lesser extent, Certeau. The question then is whether they are capable of contributing to a more adequate construction of the popular, and one which can account for the social interests involved in the deployment of the category.

The crucial issue here is that of the coherence of the category of 'the people', and particularly its problematic relation to the category of class. It is not just that the content of the concept of 'the people' is historically variable, but that it depends for all its force on a deliberate vagueness of reference—and such a vagueness certainly characterizes Hall's use of it. Although he speaks of 'the oppressed, the excluded classes' as the core of the 'popular', the concept refers more broadly to the possibility of a shifting alliance of whatever classes are in opposition to 'the power bloc' (which, again, is not a 'whole' class but a cultural-political formation). What happens here is that the category of class is reserved more or less exclusively for talking about relations within the economic sphere, whereas 'the people' and 'the power bloc' are seen as the appropriate terms for describing conflict on the terrains of culture and politics (including questions of gender and race).[27] The point of the concept of the popular, Hall writes, is that it is not pre-given in economic relations but is culturally and politically constructed (the product of a deliberately political interest): 'The capacity to *constitute* classes and individuals as a popular force—that is the nature of political and cultural struggle: to *make* the divided classes and the separated peoples—divided and separated by culture as much as by other factors—*into* a popular-democratic cultural force' (p. 239), and in particular to contest the ground lost to an apparently triumphant Thatcherism in the 1980s. The price paid for this separation of the economic (the sphere

[27] 'The people versus the power-bloc: this, rather than "class against class," is the central line of contradiction around which the terrain of culture is polarized' (p. 238).

of class relations) from the cultural and political is, however, a real difficulty in understanding what it is that connects them.

Hall's conception of the popular is deeply indebted to Ernesto Laclau's work on populism. In order to clarify the dimensions of the problem, let me turn to Laclau's exposition of the relations between class and the category of the popular, especially as it is developed in *Politics and Ideology in Marxist Theory*.[28] His account begins with the difficulty of describing the historical phenomenon of populism in class-based terms, since different populist movements have had widely disparate class characteristics; yet, he says, one can only begin to analyse the phenomenon by seeking the class contradictions on which populist movements are built. Laclau seeks to resolve this aporia by distinguishing between the *fact* of the class determination of political and ideological structures, and the particular 'forms of existence' of classes at the level of these superstructures—that is, the variety of different forms in which determination (or 'limitation', as Raymond Williams would put it) is manifested. This is a refusal of the view that 'every ideological and political element has a *necessary* class belonging' (p. 159), and that some sort of class essence is thus expressed in every cultural form or political practice. If, on the contrary, we suppose that classes can act and express themselves in a large number of ways which are not predetermined by their class character, then we can say that the political and class import of a particular ideology is given only by its specific articulation with other ideologies at a particular moment in time.

The point of this argument is to make it possible to understand the hegemony of a ruling class, and indeed all class action, as being structured and sustained by a complex of ideological and political relations that are relatively independent of the logic of economic production (and so of class relations strictly speaking). The concept of 'the people'

[28] Ernesto Laclau, *Politics and Ideology in Marxist Theory: Capitalism—Fascism—Populism* (London: Verso, 1977). References will be incorporated in the text.

corresponds to this set of contingencies, and the political/ cultural action that forges and consolidates class power can only be understood in relation to it: 'Classes cannot assert their hegemony without articulating the people in their discourse; and the specific form of this articulation in the case of a class which seeks to confront the power bloc as a whole, in order to assert its hegemony, will be populism' (p. 196). This is a distinction, then, between two different conceptual levels: the 'abstract' level of the mode of production, and the 'concrete' level of the social formation (pp. 107–8). To phrase the distinction in this way is more or less akin to writing off the concept of class as irrelevant to real social struggles (apart from strictly economic conflict), where instead it is the formation of disparate groups into a generalized opposition between 'the people' and 'the power bloc' that bears the force of social contradiction. One can still speak of class struggle, but at the political and ideological levels it consists for the most part in an attempt to win popular allegiance through the clash of antagonistic discourses. This invocation (or 'interpellation') of popular allegiance

not only has no precise class content, but is the domain of ideological class struggle par excellence. Every class struggles at the ideological level *simultaneously* as class and as people, or rather, tries to give coherence to its ideological discourse by presenting its class objectives as the consummation of popular objectives.   (pp. 108–9)

'The people' is thus not a liberal or idealist term extraneous to Marxism; it is the very form of all class struggle, and indeed as a phenomenon it is of longer duration and greater stability than particular historical classes.[29] It is also, and crucially, the

---

[29] Laclau writes that, since '"popular traditions" constitute the complex of interpellations which express the "people"/power bloc contradiction as distinct from a class contradiction', so 'in so far as "popular traditions" represent the ideological crystallization of resistance to oppression in general, that is, *to the very form of the State*, they will be longer lasting than class ideologies and will constitute a structural frame of reference of greater stability' (p. 167). This seems to me to accept at face value the ideological function of the concept of 'the people'—that is, the blurring of precise class differentiations—and, in particular, to open up a dubious continuity with traditions of peasant (or 'folk') revolt.

form in which the *polarization* of the social order becomes possible. Here the key distinction, which is more fully developed in later texts (many written with Chantal Mouffe), is that between 'democratic' and 'popular' position-alities.

The democratic subject position, which occupies that space that we conventionally think of as the political, is the locus of a particular, clearly delimited antagonism; it is the local form of difference experienced by any dominated group (a subordinate class, women, an oppressed racial community, marginalized groups of various kinds), and it is the place where 'subjectivity is constructed through the contradictory play of power and resistance to power'.[30] The popular subject position, by contrast, involves the linking up of different democratic positions to form a complex articulation. The basis for this welding together of diverse groups is the construction of chains of equivalence between them, in such a way that dispersed relations of subordination are transformed into a unified set of relations of oppression, predicated on the recognition of a generalized wrong. The category of 'the people' is the effect of this reorganization of the whole field of the social into an antagonistic duality.

To these two forms of subject position correspond two different forms of political mobilization, and two distinct structures of social contradiction. On the one hand, populist antagonism is, in formal terms, a relation to the Other and a discourse of otherness, and it supposes 'a relation in which the reality of one pole is purely and simply the negation of the other'.[31] It is that 'failure of difference' in which I can conceive of my Other only metaphorically, as 'a symbol of my non-being'.[32] Its logic of equivalence is 'a logic of the

[30] Ernesto Laclau, '"Socialism", the "People", "Democracy": The Trans-formation of Hegemonic Logic', *Social Text*, 7 (Spring/Summer 1983), 118.

[31] Ernesto Laclau, 'Populist Rupture and Discourse', *Screen Education*, 34 (1980), 90.

[32] Ernesto Laclau and Chantal Mouffe, *Hegemony and Socialist Strategy: Towards a Radical Democratic Politics*, trans. Winston Moore and Paul Cammack (London: Verso, 1985), 125.

simplification of political space', whereas the logic of difference that organizes the democratic position 'is a logic of its expansion and increasing complexity'.[33] It is, then, the construction of antagonistic chains of equivalence that makes possible a rupture of the social system and the establishment of a new hegemony, whereas the logic of dispersed differences allows only adjustment to the system and the integration of complexity.

The force of Laclau's uncompromisingly binarist rhetoric is to make perfectly clear the political consequences of a populist model of struggle. The logic of antagonism is, evidently, a specular logic, in which I construct my Other through a structure of inverse sameness, as I construct my alliances through an abolition of real diversity. The 'failure of difference' of which Laclau and Mouffe explicitly speak indicates that, in this model, the concept of the popular operates in the pre-symbolic domain of a phantasy of counter-identification with the Other, a Master/Slave dialectic in which each position is structurally reversible. It is this that constitutes the model's efficacy, but only at the price of a repetition of the Same: on this interpretation, populist antagonism can never break the cycle of power because it is never more than its mirror image.

Everything hinges on the argument that only a populist organization of the social will have the capacity to identify the power bloc as its antagonist and to unite oppressed social groups in a starkly defined struggle. But of course what is at stake here is not directly the power bloc but rather a particular discursive *representation* of the power bloc. Thatcher and Reagan's identification of the State and of a 'liberal' Establishment as the locus of social power have made it obvious, if it wasn't before, that populist movements are bound up with phantasies of the Other that have no necessary connection to the realities of class control (Frederick Pollack observes neatly that 'under Reagan, the term *Washington*—in

[33] Ernesto Laclau and Chantal Mouffe, *Hegemony and Socialist Strategy: Towards a Radical Democratic Politics*, 130.

the minds of middle- and working-class people who agreed that it meant "the enemy"—referred to minorities, the poor, intellectuals, and liberals');[34] populism has no inherently socialist form, and at its extreme right-wing populism merges with fascism.

Laclau understands this ambivalence, of course (his formative experience was of Peronism, one of the most profoundly unstable and unpredictable of populisms),[35] and he tries to avoid it by distinguishing between 'a populism of the dominant classes and a populism of the dominated classes'.[36] But the problem lies not in the particular inflection given to a populist movement (and typically, in any case, such movements combine both left- and right-wing characteristics), but in the 'structure of feeling' that organizes it: the building of a space of equivalences held together by the absolute otherness of the opponent; the repression of difference; the politics of the Imaginary.[37]

It is in this sense that the model of the popular developed by Laclau and taken over in all essential respects by Stuart Hall seems to me unusable either for scholarly work or for a socialist politics. Its key weakness is that it surrenders the precision of a multi-layered class analysis, and it does so because Laclau and Mouffe can conceive of class only as a function of the system of relations of production. More precisely, since the concept of relations of production in principle refers to *any* social relations that support production (and they all do), they conceive class strictly speaking only in terms of the technical division of labour. The paradox of this avowedly anti-essentialist vision of class is that it rests upon the most economistic and reductionist understanding: rather

[34] Frederick Pollack, 'Theses on Intellectuals', *Representations*, 39 (Summer 1992), 73.
[35] Cf. the 'intellectual biography' in *New Reflections on the Revolution of our Time* (London: Verso, 1990), 197–204.
[36] Laclau, *Politics and Ideology in Marxist Theory*, 87.
[37] Cf. Julia Kristeva, 'Women's Time', *The Kristeva Reader*, ed. Toril Moi (Oxford: Basil Blackwell, 1986), 203: 'The very logic of counter-power and of counter-society necessarily generates, by its very structure, its essence as a simulacrum of the combated society or of power.'

than defining class in terms of positions worked out (although not, of course, pre-given) across the whole spectrum of the social, they flatten it to a single dimension. As Chantal Mouffe says in a joint interview with Laclau (I am assuming that the collaboration authorizes my treating them as a single authorial subject):

We can use the concept of class to designate positions at the level of the relations of production, but in that case we cannot deduce from it anything necessary concerning politics or ideology. Or, we can reserve the term to designate collectivities in struggle at the political level and whose objectives include the transformation of the relations of production. But in this case we cannot know anything necessary concerning the position of those agents in the process of production.[38]

Again, it is the *connections* between production and culture that are severed in this model of class. If there are no necessary consequences of an agent's place in production, then there can be no way of grounding political action in social interest and indeed no reason (except contingent or 'ethical' reasons) for supporting one group against another. The concept of the people, with its deliberate blurring of class and other distinctions (could we not say that its primary function since the French Revolution has been to screen particular class interests?) and its drastic simplification of the political space, is a poor substitute for the complex discriminations offered by a properly multi-dimensional class analysis.

What are the consequences of rejecting the category of the popular (in the sense in which I have defined it here)? Let me stress, as forcefully as I can, that what is being rejected is *not* the heterogeneous space of texts and practices covered by the term, nor is it the political impulse to recover and to give value to the domain of everyday culture; such a ' "siding" for or against the "popular" ', as Meaghan Morris writes, would be

[38] 'Recasting Marxism: Hegemony and New Political Movements', Interview with Ernesto Laclau and Chantal Mouffe, *Socialist Review* 66, Vol. 12, No. 6 (Nov–Dec. 1982), 107.

'a quite pointless manoeuvre'.[39] My refusal is only of the categories, or more precisely the *structure* of the categories, used to construct and to describe this space. This is equally, then, a refusal of the category of 'high' culture, either in the sense of a domain of self-evident value or in the sense of a set of texts and practices necessarily and expressively linked to a dominant class; and it is, of course, a refusal of that tradition of moralizing or patronizing evaluation of 'low' culture in relation to 'high' culture which stretches from modernism's self-definition in relation to its mass-cultural Other through to various defences of the popular (in Hoggart and the early Williams, for example, or in the folkloric tradition) as being aesthetically 'valid' in its own right, or as an 'authentic' expression of class or community.

Equally, this is not to argue that the concept of the popular may not have a strategic value in certain circumstances: it may work effectively as a slogan in struggles against oligarchic forms of power, and it continues to be useful in breaking down rigidly canonical structures in traditional curricula; judgements about its value will have a different force in different national contexts (thus Andrew Ross notes that wearing a Coca Cola T-shirt works in the Third World as at once an index of cultural imperialism and a promise of modernity).[40] More importantly, perhaps, to refuse the category of the popular as a valid *descriptive* category shouldn't mean that we overlook its continuing function in organizing perceptions of how the cultural space is structured: it performs a definite ideological work in differentiating cultural production and reception into disparate and indeed incompatible spheres which carry real differences of value for their respective audiences and readerships. The point is to describe this normative structure rather than to accept it as a given.

The untenable core of the concept of the popular (or of the 'mass'-cultural) is its structural opposition to high culture: a

[39] Meaghan Morris, 'At Henry Parkes Motel', *Cultural Studies*, 2: 1 (1988), 34.
[40] Ross, *No Respect*, 8.

binarism which at once unifies and differentiates each domain. The category of popular culture has a unitary form, however, only as long as it is derived from a singular entity, 'the people'; otherwise it breaks down into a bundle of very heterogeneous forms and practices. Its appearance of unity is reinforced by the privileging of certain key examples: in the folkloric tradition it is the practices of song, dance, speech, and storytelling occurring outside commercial mediation that take this privilege; in cultural studies it is youth subcultures, which in practice means an exclusive focus on urban, public, and, as McRobbie notes, male cultural forms.[41] Such accounts are of course implicitly normative (reggae, hip-hop, and scratch video are given a status which is denied to Val Doonican, Kenny Rogers, and family sitcoms). It may ultimately be important to argue for such normative distinctions, but it is surely crucial in the first instance to recognize the sheer diversity of the field drawn together by the term 'popular': it ranges from home movies to access television to studio-produced programming; from spiritualist groups to trade union seminars; from home gardening to pornography; from beach cricket to organized professional football; and from heavy metal to the Reader's Digest.

As the term is currently structured, the 'popular' is understood as the emanation of a homogeneous popular will, a singular politico-cultural impulse that feeds into and

[41] Angela McRobbie, 'Settling Accounts with Subcultures: A Feminist Critique', *Screen Education*, 34 (1980), 37–49. In a later article ('Dance and Social Fantasy', in Angela McRobbie and Mica Nava (eds.), *Gender and Generation* (London: Macmillan, 1984), 141) McRobbie points to the way youth culture is conceived entirely in terms of the public domain (school, the dole, the street) and of direct experience. This has the effect 'of reducing the entire spectrum of young people's experience implicitly to these moments, neglecting almost totally those many times where they become viewers, readers, part of an audience, or simply silent, caught up in their own daydreams. To ignore these is to miss an absolutely central strand in their social and personal experience. It means that in all these subcultural accounts we are left with little knowledge of any one of their reading or viewing experiences, and therefore with how they find themselves represented in these texts, and with how in turn they appropriate from some of these and discard others. This absence has also produced a real blindness to the debt much of those youth cultural expressions owe to literary texts, to the cinema, to art and to older musical forms.'

through the cultural forms adapted to its expression. The concept articulates the social into a single contradiction, and then imagines this contradiction through a pathos of repression.

In formal terms, the expressive or possessive relation of the people to the popular is given either by right of production or by right of appropriation (and transformation). The former would tend to privilege forms of 'folk' production (quiltmaking or bush ballads or joke-telling) and fails to account adequately for the 'mass'-cultural forms industrially produced by middle-class knowledge-workers within cultural apparatuses owned either by private capital or by the State. Any immediate read-off of political function and cultural value from the position of this class is problematic because of its structural ambivalence: as I argued in relation to Bourdieu's work, the middle-class intelligentsia has its own specificity and cannot be claimed directly either for the dominant class or 'the people'. But to define the popular in terms of forms of appropriation (popular regimes of reading, the subversive and 'tactical' ruses of consumption that Certeau describes) has the theoretical drawback of supposing that a set of dominated classes has developed quite separate and autonomous practices of reading from those employed by a dominant class: that the popular, far from being the site of the struggle for hegemony, has escaped all hegemonic influence.[42]

---

[42] Tony Bennett argues that both the 'structuralist' and the 'culturalist' paradigms in cultural studies 'regard the sphere of cultural and ideological practices as being governed by a dominant ideology, essentially and monolithically bourgeois in its characteristics, which, albeit with varying degrees of success, is imposed from without, as an alien force, on the subordinate classes'. Both of these approaches see the cultural field as 'divided between two opposing cultural and ideological camps—bourgeois and working class—locked in a zero-sum game in which one side gains only at the expense of the other and in which the ultimate objective is the liquidation of one by the other so that the victor might then stand in the place of the vanquished' ('Introduction: Popular Culture and "the Turn to Gramsci"', in Tony Bennett, Colin Mercer, and Janet Woollacott (eds.), *Popular Culture and Social Relations* (Milton Keynes: Open University Press, 1986), pp. xiii–xiv). Against this he sets the thesis that 'it is no more possible in the past than in the present to locate a source of popular cultural activity or expression which is not, at the same time, profoundly shot through

One way of undermining the expressive unity of the concept while still recognizing its continuing discursive force as a vehicle for the self-recognition and self-identification of diverse social groups is to argue that 'the people' is not a given entity which precedes cultural forms, but is rather entirely the product of cultural forms: that it is a fact of representation rather than an external cause of representation. The corollary of this is that contemporary culture industries work hard to construct their audience as 'the people'.[43] Noel King and Tim Rowse, analysing the genre of 'humanity ads' on Australian television (advertisements representing the common humanity of a mosaic of diverse individuals, as members of a national community or a community of consumers of a product or a community of viewers of a particular station), have noticed that the structure of identification set up in these ads is based in 'the consistent appeal to endorse the ordinary as authentic and shared'. In their specifically patriotic mode the ads 'avoid politics and go straight to the people as the source and addressee of their message', and this structure of address can be generalized: in all such advertisements, but also as the most

with elements of the dominant culture and, in some sense, located within it as well as against it. That is what a dominant culture does: it dominates, it constitutes the magnetic pole of the cultural field which other cultures may oppose or seek to disentangle themselves from, but which they cannot evade entirely' ('The Politics of "the Popular" and Popular Culture', ibid. 18).

[43] On the concept of audience as methodological fiction, cf. Lawrence Grossberg, 'The Context of Audiences and the Politics of Difference', *Australian Journal of Communication*, 16 (1989), 16: 'There is no real audience waiting out there to be constructed; the "audience" is not only a theoretical abstraction, but, at the present moment, a rather chaotic one'. John Hartley writes that 'audiences are not just constructs; they are the invisible fictions that are produced institutionally in order for various institutions to take charge of the mechanisms of their own survival. Audiences may be imagined empirically, theoretically or politically, but in all cases the product is a fiction that serves the needs of the imagining institution. In no case is the audience "real", or external to its discursive construction. There is no "actual" audience that lies beyond its production as a category, which is merely to say that audiences are only ever encountered *per se* as *representations*. Furthermore, they are so rarely *self-represented* that they are almost always absent.' 'Invisible Fictions: Television Audiences, Paedocracy, Pleasure', *Textual Practice*, 1: 2 (Summer 1987), 125; cf. also John Hartley, 'The Real World of Audiences', *Critical Studies in Mass Communication* (Sept. 1988), 234–8. Both essays are reprinted in John Hartley, *Tele-ology: Studies in Television* (London: Routledge, 1992), 101–25.

general form of television enunciation (other foregrounded instances would be the tribunary figure of the anchorperson, or the voxpop interview, or the telethon), 'it is the public which speaks to itself, powerfully implying a less authentic public world of politics and media hype that is elsewhere and ultimately unnecessary'.[44] Employing a repertoire of plebiscitary strategies, the broadcast media mobilize 'a sense of the common (but individually differentiated) detachment of the daily life of ordinary people from the official duties and formally-defined institutional life of society' (p. 41); 'the people' are constructed in being spoken for.[45]

In arguing for a more complex correlation of social position with cultural practice I nevertheless retain Bourdieu's key thesis: that the primary business of culture is distinction, the stratification of tastes in such a way as to construct and reinforce differentiations of social status which correspond, *in historically variable and often highly mediated ways*, to achieved or aspired-to class position. Cultural discrimination involves a constant negotiation of position with the aim of naturalizing one's own set of values, distinguishing them from the values of others, and attempting more or less forcefully to impose one's values on others. It is thus not just a matter of self-definition but also of struggle for social legitimation.

Whereas in highly stratified societies culture is closely tied to class structure, in most advanced capitalist societies the cultural system is no longer organized in a strict hierarchy and is no longer *in the same manner* tense with the play of power.

[44] Noel King and Tim Rowse, '"Typical Aussies": Television and Populism in Australia', *Framework*, 22–3 (Autumn 1983), 39. Further references will be given in the text.

[45] Cf. Simon Frith's argument that 'popular culture produces "the people", not vice versa. . . . What seems to be involved here is not identification as such (between fan and star, say) but a process of *recognition*, in which cultural form—tones of voice, jokiness, parody, a self-conscious distancing, *play* with relationships of fantasy and reality—is as important as cultural content. . . . The most important ideological role of capitalist culture is to mobilize people to vote or to buy by "placing" them, giving them a social identity through popular taste.' Simon Frith, 'Hearing Secret Harmonies', in Colin MacCabe (ed.), *High Culture/ Low Culture: Analysing Popular Television and Film* (New York: St Martin's Press, 1986), 53–70.

This is so in particular because of the mediation of two cultural institutions: that of the mass media, which construct heterogeneous global audiences rather than class-specific audiences; and that of the mass education system, which, rather than being directly tied to the reproduction of an élite, now has the more diffuse function of the differential formation of cultural capital. Between them, these institutions have thoroughly transformed the system of 'postmodern' relations of cultural value. Bill Schwarz puts it this way:

We are coming to a time when the model which describes popular culture in a relation of antagonism to a high or elite culture is, in some senses, ceasing to be serviceable. The reason for this has precisely to do with the dynamics of popular culture as a capitalist culture. For the great commodification of popular culture which coincided with what is variously described as mass society, monopoly capitalism, or the modernist epoch has had the effect, in subsequent decades, of eroding high culture as a determining field of force, just as the pessimists of the 1930s had feared. This is not to say that high culture has disappeared. It is merely to note that it no longer is able to exert the same force throughout the social formation, its authenticity no longer able to secure universal respect, its place taken—across classes—by mainstream pop music, TV soaps, the blockbuster movie, and so on. Capital accumulation has never exhibited much respect for traditions inherited from previous formations, and this applies to traditional intellectuals as much as to anything else.[46]

High culture, we might say, is no longer 'the dominant culture' but is rather a *pocket* within commodity culture. Its primary relationship is not to the ruling class but to the intelligentsia, and to the education system which is the locus of their power and the generative point for most high-cultural practices.[47] And, like 'popular' culture, it can incorporate any number of quite heterogeneous aesthetic texts—from Jean

[46] Bill Schwarz, 'Popular Culture: The Long March', *Cultural Studies*, 3: 2 (1989), 254–5.

[47] Although here we should distinguish between those practices which are still quite closely tied to upper-class status and to the family, such as ballet, opera, and perhaps the theatre, and the more 'rootless' practices of art, literature, and film.

Renoir to John Waters, from Palestrina to fusion rock, from Racine to Kathy Acker.

What follows from this dispersal of the categories of a 'high' and a 'popular' culture may indeed be the end of one kind of story about the organization of culture; that story, in both its conservative and its oppositional forms, was predicated on the fixity of cultural norms and the essential coherence of cultural 'levels'. From another perspective, however, what follows then is not an end but a beginning. We are not finished with the categories of the 'high' and the 'popular', but must construct them in a quite different way.

If the foregoing critique of the concept of the popular is not to be taken as a pretext for abandoning the field to which the concept refers, then two conditions, it seems to me, must be met. In the first place, the analysis of cultural texts must be set in relation to the institutionalized regimes of value that sustain them and that organize them in relations of difference and distinction. (The concept of regime of value is theorized more fully in the final chapter.) And, second, our attention must be turned away from that mythical popular subject immediate to observation, and focused instead on the *relation between* two different kinds of practice: a 'first-order' practice of everyday culture, and the 'second-order' practice of analysis of it conducted by a reader endowed with significant cultural capital. I define this here, and for my present purposes, as a relation between intellectuals and their others—whoever those 'others' may be, and recognizing that these two groups, and these two kinds of practice, often and perhaps necessarily overlap ('first-order' practices are also reflexive; intellectuals are themselves those 'others'). It is the politics of this relation that must frame any reading of cultural texts 'in themselves'.[48]

---

[48] The Birmingham Popular Memory Group has similar things to say in this respect about the relation between historian and 'source' in the recording of oral history. Popular Memory Group, 'Popular Memory: Theory, Politics, Method', in Richard Johnson *et al.* (eds.), *Making Histories: Studies in History-Writing and Politics* (Minneapolis: University of Minnesota Press, 1982), esp. 220, 243, 251.

In order to understand the de-centred structure of the system of cultural value it becomes crucial, then, to analyse the specificity of the class of intellectuals: that is, of the category of cultural capital and its place in the system of production. This is the task of my next chapter.

3

Class and Cultural Capital

Capitalism is one of the names modernity goes by. It consisted in the retraction of the infinite into an instance that had already been designated by Descartes (and perhaps by Augustine, the first modern): the will. . . . Capitalism posits the infinite as that which is not yet determined, as that which the will must indefinitely master and appropriate. The infinite bears the names of cosmos, energy, and research and development. . . . The decisive factor in what is called the postindustrial (Touraine, Bell) is that the infinity of the will invests language itself. The major development of the last twenty years, expressed in the most vapid terms of political economy and historical periodization, has been the transformation of language into a productive commodity: phrases considered as messages to encode, decode, transmit, and order (by the bundle), to reproduce, conserve, and keep available (memories), to combine and conclude (calculations), and to oppose (games, conflicts, cybernetics); and the establishment of a unit of measure that is also a price unit, in other words, information. The effects of the penetration of capitalism into language are just beginning to be felt. Beneath the surface of market expansion and a new industrial strategy, the coming century will be characterized by the investment of the desire for the infinite in language transactions, following the criterion of maximum performativity.[1]

The work of intellectuals is the implementation of modernity.

[1] Jean-François Lyotard, 'Rules and Paradoxes and Svelte Appendix', trans. Brian Massumi, *Cultural Critique*, 5 (Winter 1986–7), 215, 217.

By 'intellectuals' I do not mean the 'traditional' or 'high' intelligentsia: the small élite of men and women of letters who act as public spokespersons for the 'noble' disciplines of knowledge (philosophy, the arts, the social sciences, the higher natural sciences). Rather, following Gramsci,[2] I mean all of those whose work is socially defined as being based upon the possession and exercise of knowledge, whether that knowledge be prestigious or routine, technical or speculative. (This definition will be made more precise in the course of this chapter.) Unless this broader and socially relational categorization is adopted, it seems to me that any account of the stratum or class of intellectuals can only be a moralizing exercise in self-hatred and self-idealization.[3]

The work of intellectuals comprises a set of historically defined tasks, which I summarize, in Foucault's terms, as a mode of 'governmental' regulation that makes all domains of life, including both the 'public' domain of work and the realm of the 'private' whose borders it defines and patrols, visible to the scrutiny and the calculations of power. ('Power' here includes but is not restricted to the State.) Its instrument and medium is a culture of enlightened discourse which mobilizes a historically specific apparatus of power and knowledge around the claim to truth. And it is grounded in a set of economic conditions which make possible the constitution of

[2] Gramsci's understanding of intellectuals is built around the interplay between the universality of intellectual activity and the historical specialization of intellectual functions, which are bound up, either directly or indirectly, with the establishment of class hegemony. Intellectual work is thus not defined by its intrinsic characteristics but by its place within a complex ensemble of social relations. Antonio Gramsci, *Selections from the Prison Notebooks*, ed. and trans. Quintin Hoare and Geoffrey Nowell-Smith (London: Lawrence and Wishart, 1971), esp. 5–13.

[3] Subtle and cogent as much of it is, Zygmunt Bauman's argument in *Legislators and Interpreters* and elsewhere is ultimately flawed by its attribution to intellectuals (meaning 'traditional' intellectuals) of the autonomy and effective social power that they have claimed for themselves. Zygmunt Bauman, *Legislators and Interpreters: On Modernity, Post-modernity and Intellectuals* (Cambridge: Polity Press, 1987). In this respect it repeats the various right-wing versions of the critique, which dissociate the 'New Class' from the real embeddedness of knowledge in capitalist production. Cf. the essays by Daniel Bell, Jeane Kirkpatrick, Norman Podhoretz, and others in B. Bruce-Briggs (ed.), *The New Class?* (New Brunswick, NJ: Transaction Press, 1979).

the intelligentsia as a class, or a class fraction (I leave this alternative open for the time being). These conditions are, in brief, the structural possibility of converting knowledge into cultural capital.

To speak of cultural capital is to invoke the history of the integration of knowledge into commodity production—the establishment of knowledge as a central productive force. Lyotard speaks of the 'banality' of the thesis that commodified knowledge 'has become the principal force of production over the last few decades';[4] but it is perhaps only when we understand the dimensions of this development that we can understand, on the one hand, the internal contradictions of enlightened rationality, and on the other the social interests that are invested in the sphere of disinterested reason, and thus the particular range of class interests that define the intelligentsia.

Let me briefly outline some of the available information about the capitalist transformation of knowledge into a productive resource, relying in particular on Fritz Machlup's *The Production and Distribution of Knowledge in the United States*[5] and on the nine-volume report, *The Information Economy*, compiled by Marc Uri Porat.[6] Machlup's is the broader definition of knowledge; his use of the category has provoked considerable criticism,[7] but the value of his analysis

[4] Jean-François Lyotard, *The Post-Modern Condition: A Report on Knowledge*, trans. Geoff Bennington and Brian Massumi, Theory and History of Literature, Vol. 10 (Minneapolis: University of Minnesota Press, 1984), 5.

[5] Fritz Machlup, *The Production and Distribution of Knowledge in the United States* (Princeton, NJ: Princeton University Press, 1962); this volume is expanded and supplemented by the three published volumes of *Knowledge: Its Creation, Distribution and Economic Significance*: Fritz Machlup, *Knowledge and Knowledge Production* (Princeton, NJ: Princeton University Press, 1980); Fritz Machlup, *The Branches of Learning* (Princeton, NJ: Princeton University Press, 1982); Fritz Machlup, *The Economics of Information and Human Capital* (Princeton, NJ: Princeton University Press, 1984). The series is completed by Michael Rogers Rubin and Mary Taylor Huber, *The Knowledge Industry in the United States, 1960–1980* (Princeton, NJ: Princeton University Press, 1986).

[6] Marc Uri Porat, *The Information Economy*, Special Publication 77–12, 9 vols. (Washington, DC: Office of Telecommunications, 1977).

[7] Porat uses a more orthodox form of accounting (the National Income Account system devised by the US Department of Commerce) and works with 'value added' rather than 'final demand' figures; this means that items which don't

is precisely that by refusing to restrict the concept of knowledge to its traditional qualitative definition (referring, in Daniel Bell's words, only to 'research . . . higher education, and the production of knowledge . . . as an intellectual property, which involves valid new knowledge and its dissemination'),[8] he is able to get at the full extent of what might be counted and costed as knowledge in a modern economy—and can thereby get at real qualitative shifts in the structure of capital and the structure of social class.

Machlup's major categories are education, research and development, media of communication, information machines, and information services. I summarize his categories and his findings as follows:

The category of education includes education in the home, in the Church, and in the armed services, on-the-job training, and elementary, secondary, and tertiary education. The tables referring to this category show a rise in enrolments in elementary and secondary schools in the years 1890–1960 from 78.1% to 95.6% of the school-age group (all figures refer to the United States), and of per capita expenditure (in constant dollars) from $2.54 to $103.38. Enrolments in higher education (1870–1960) rose from 1.7% to 33.5% of the 18–21 age group, and per capita expenditure from $0.60 to $34.59.[9]

Research and development expenditure is roughly estimated at $80 million in 1920, $130 million in 1930, $377 million in 1940, $2,870 million in 1950, and $14,000 million in 1960. This represents a growth in the 20 years to 1960 of 3,714%. Expenditure relative to GNP is 0.09% in 1920, 0.14% in 1930, 0.37% in 1940, 1.01% in 1950, and 2.78% in 1960. Government has played a central role in this growth. *(pp. 155–6)*

show up in the national accounts (such as the 'earnings forgone' by mothers educating their pre-school children, or by students) cannot be entered into the calculation of the economic costs of knowledge.

[8] Daniel Bell, *The Coming of Postindustrial Society: A Venture in Social Forecasting* (New York: Basic Books, 1973), 213.

[9] Machlup, *The Production and Distribution of Knowledge in the US*, 71–9; further references to this volume will be incorporated in the text.

The category of media of communication includes printed matter, photography and phonography, stage and cinema, broadcasting, advertising and public relations, telephone, telegraph, and postal services, and conventions *(pp. 207–94)*. These media show complex variations in growth according to their closeness to financial and industrial functions.

The category of information machines includes instruments, office information machines, and computers, with the beginnings of a massive growth in computer sales in the late 1950s just registering in Machlup's tables. *(pp. 295–322)*

The final category, information services, includes professional knowledge services (legal, engineering, architectural, accounting, medical); information and financial services (cheque-deposit banking, security and commodity brokers, insurance, and real estate); the intelligence service of wholesale traders; miscellaneous industries (business consultancies, etc.); knowledge transmission services (mailing, duplicating, etc.) and two-way transmission (credit bureaux, employment exchanges, auctioneers); and government as a knowledge industry (the state bureaucracy). *(pp. 323–53)*

The value of output for different knowledge industries in 1958 was:

education:	$60,194 million
research and development	$10,990 million
media of communication	$38,369 million
information machines	$ 8,922 million
information services	$17,961 million

The total value of output was $136,436 million, paid for 27.8% by government, 30.9% by business, and 41.3% by consumers. Total knowledge production in 1958 was almost 29% of adjusted GNP *(pp. 354–62)*, rising to 31.0% in 1963, 33.3% in 1967, 33.9% in 1972, 34.7% in 1977, and 36.5% in 1980.[10] (Porat's figures are even higher—he classifies 46.2% of GNP as information activity, and 53% of all income as earned by information workers.)[11]

---

[10] Rubin and Huber, *The Knowledge Industry in the US.*

[11] Marc Uri Porat, *The Information Economy*, Vol. 1: *Definition and Measurement*, p. 7, Table 1.1, 'The Structure of the Information Economy (1967)'.

Of particular significance are the shifts in the workforce measured in Machlup's Table X-2, 'Labour Force: Percentage Distribution over Broad Occupation Categories, 1900–1959' *(p. 382)*:

Category	1900	1910	1920	1930	1940	1950	1959
White Collar	17.6	21.3	24.9	29.4	31.1	36.6	42.1
Manual/Service	44.9	47.7	48.1	49.4	51.5	51.6	48.0
Farm	37.5	30.9	27.0	21.2	17.4	11.8	9.9

The table is continued by Rubin and Huber as follows:

Category	1958	1963	1967	1972	1977	1980
White Collar	43.0	45.6	46.0	47.8	49.9	52.2
Manual/Service	48.2	47.9	49.2	48.4	47.1	45.0
Farm	8.8	6.5	4.8	3.8	3.0	2.8 [12]

After a more detailed analysis of these figures into occupations producing or not producing knowledge, Machlup summarizes the trends read from the statistical series as follows: '(1) The knowledge-producing occupations have grown over the last sixty years much faster than occupations requiring manual labour. (2) The share of knowledge-producing occupations in the total labour force tripled between 1900 and 1959. (3) The share of these occupations in total employment has increased even more. (4) While in the first part of this century growth was fastest in clerical occupations, the lead was then taken by managerial and executive occupations, and more recently by professional and technical personnel. (5) The share of knowledge-producing occupations in total income has increased during the last decade. (6) The share of professional and technical personnel in total income has increased during the last two decades.' In general: 'The changing employment pattern

[12] Rubin and Huber, *The Knowledge Industry in the US*, 195.

indicates a continuing movement from manual to mental, and from less to more highly trained labour.' *(pp. 396–7)*

These conclusions are very general and do little more than provide a statistical basis for a widely accepted understanding of changes in the workforce of the advanced capitalist economies.[13] What they don't conceptualize is the reasons for the increased productivity of the 'knowledge-producing occupations': that is, they offer no theory of the historical change in the composition of capital, and indeed of how it might be possible to understand knowledge as a *form* of capital. The starting point for such a theory might be an understanding that knowledge is a moment of both capital and labour, and can be translated into each of these categories (as indeed they are constantly translated into each other); the productivity of knowledge could thus be thought on the one hand as an increase in the proportion of constant to variable capital, on the other as a 'rising proportion of embodied to direct labour'.[14] Such a theorization would require a disruption of the Marxist opposition, fundamental to the labour theory of value and founded in an anthropology that privileges the immediacy of human work over its mediate

[13] Fukio Kodama, for example, has spoken of a 'paradigm change' in the corporation, from being 'a place for production' to being 'a place for thinking', and compiles figures to show that in the sixty-eight major Japanese manufacturing companies, 'R & D investment surpassed traditional capital investment, on average, from 1987'. Fukio Kodama, 'How Investment Decisions Are Made in Japanese Industry', in D. Evered and S. Harnett (eds.), *The Evaluation of Scientific Research* (London: J. Wiley, 1987), 201.

[14] Adam Westoby, 'Mental Work, Education, and the Division of Labour', in Ron Eyerman, Lennart G. Svensson, and Thomas Söderqvist (eds.), *Intellectuals, Universities, and the State in Western Modern Societies* (Berkeley: University of California Press, 1987), 130; Westoby adds that there are 'two general trends that increase the ratio of educated labour: first, its increasing share as an input, both as research and development and through the increasing relative weight of the control functions of organization and administration; and second, preceding these, the increasing proportion of labour which is employed (largely by the state) in maintaining and reproducing the labourers, the population, and the social organism (e.g., health and social services, education, and civil and social administration). Together, these trends mean that the production of both labour and other goods is becoming more and more intensive of educated labour. If, then, we speak of the rise of a knowledge class, it must be understood that its origins lie as much in production as in distribution or in control over it' (p. 131).

transformations, between 'living' and 'dead', direct and indirect, immediate and stored labour: *knowledge is stored labour which is productive*. And it would have to move beyond the *sociological* level of an analysis of patterns of change in occupational proportions, since 'the underlying transformation consists not simply of a shift in the proportion of people who have specialized knowledge but also of the new centrality of the structures of socially objectified knowledge'.[15]

Machlup's conclusions, and even more the methodological framework from which they are derived, do, however, seem to me to prepare the way for a class-based account of the work of intellectuals which would be broadly Gramscian in its refusal to separate valued from disvalued knowledges.[16] In so doing they make it possible to broach the following questions:

• How is the vocational complicity of intellectuals with modernity established?

• How, if at all, does knowledge constitute the basis for a class formation?[17]

---

[15] Adam Westoby, 'Mental Work, Education, and the Division of Labour', 147.

[16] I differ from Gramsci, however, in that I attempt to relate the possession of specialized knowledges to membership of a distinct class formation rather than to already existing, economically defined classes. On this point cf. Nancy Armstrong and Leonard Tennenhouse, *The Imaginary Puritan: Literature, Intellectual Labour, and the Origins of Personal Life* (Berkeley: University of California Press, 1992), 130. Armstrong and Tennenhouse propose breaking the opposition between intellectual and 'productive' labour, not by defining intellectuals as a 'new' social class but by seeing the bourgeoisie itself (at least in England) as a class whose power was primarily based in the control of information.

[17] Note that this is not an attempt to ground a social class in a fundamental economic category. As I indicated above, the Marxist understanding of knowledge either as constant capital or—its dialectical equivalent—as stored or 'dead' labour (neither of which can create new value, and neither of which can therefore function as a productive force) is quite useless. Several interesting passages in the *Grundrisse* on machinery (the section on the concept of fixed capital at the end of Notebook VI and the beginning of Notebook VII, written in February and March of 1858) do, however, suggest the possibility that indirect labour might be capable of producing value, and that the labour theory of value, and hence the domination of capital over production, might be dissolved under technologically advanced conditions of production. Karl Marx, *Grundrisse: Foundations of the Critique of Political Economy (Rough Draft)*, trans. Martin Nicolaus (Harmondsworth: Penguin, 1973), 691–700.

- What role do cultural practices play in forming the common interests of this class, and how can we define the intelligentsia's class interests and institutional investments in the domain of culture?

These questions then in turn open out in two directions: in the one, on to the central questions of this book concerning the organization of cultural value, and particularly the relations between the categories of high and low culture; and in the other on to the *political* question of the claim of intellectuals to the right to speak on behalf of others, or on behalf of a universal reason: which is, at the last but also always from the beginning, the question of the position of interest from which I formulate these questions.

Yet there is reason to doubt whether the analysis of social class is any longer a feasible or even an interesting project (and indeed, it has been precisely a preoccupation with the knowledge classes, with the 'embarrassment' of the new middle class,[18] that has helped to undermine much of the simple explanatory power of class theory).[19] The theoretical analysis of social class has become deeply unfashionable, and for good and persuasive reasons. Briefly, they are these: that class analysis reduces political and cultural struggles and determinations, and the specific institutions through which they work, to the singular underlying logic of the economy and of places generated in economic production; that it describes social groups as essences, unified subjects with a pre-given structure of interests to which real behaviour and awareness may or may not correspond; that even when it recognizes the social effectivity of gender, race, ethnicity,

[18] Erik Olin Wright speaks of recent class analysis's 'pre-eminent preoccupation' with the '"embarrassment of the middle classes"' in *Classes* (London: Verso, 1985), 13.

[19] 'The problems in the conceptualization of class structure arise principally, although not exclusively, from the appearance of people variously termed salaried employees, white-collar workers, nonmanual workers, *ouvriers intellectuels*, service workers, technicians, "the new middle classes".' Adam Przeworski, *Capitalism and Social Democracy* (Cambridge: Cambridge University Press, 1985), 62.

regionality, age, and religion, it is constitutionally incapable of treating them as other than supplementary determinations which are to be integrated into the master code of class; and that even at its most sophisticated, it tends to be a taxonomy rather than an account of processes and interrelations.

In nevertheless pursuing here a class-based analysis of the vocation and the social capacities of intellectuals, and in exploring some of the theoretical preconditions of such an analysis, I am driven by the strong sense that in throwing out reductionist conceptions of class—and they have virtually all been reductionist—we have lost an indispensable analytic tool. We can understand neither the most delicate and subtle nor the most crude and basic movements of social power; and not only can we no longer explain crucial aspects of the role of cultural capital in production and in the exercise of political and ideological power, but we open up areas of necessary blindness towards the interests that limit, but also constitute, the power of theoretical work. Class theory is an instrument for pulling together the strands of social being, thinking it in terms of relationality (which is not the same as totality) rather than the pure dispersal of social action over a multiplicity of disconnected sites. It is never a singular instrument, since social position is always a complex knot of determinations: the choice of focus on class rather than gender or race or ethnicity will be one determined by narrative usefulness rather than by a hierarchy of theoretical models; but without it social and cultural theory is trivialized.

My expectation is that a more adequate theory of class might be able to situate the group of 'cultural' intellectuals[20] within a broader social formation made up of all those who work in the knowledge industries (all those whose income depends on possession of cultural capital); and might make it possible to identify a range of *interests* that would in some sense constrain and direct the actions and the social relations of this class or class fraction.

[20] By 'cultural intellectuals' I mean most of those in Machlup's categories one and three, education and media of communication, and who count as performing 'mental labour'.

Let me begin, then, by arguing that the various post-Marxist critiques of the category of class have been flawed by equating the concept of class with precisely the economistic and reductionist model they reject. They have been trapped in a specular relationship to Marxist orthodoxy, repeating the structure of its category of class and simply reversing the value and the explanatory force attributed to it.

The authors of a recent survey have this to say about movements in the post-Marxist theorization of class:

A curious but largely unnoticed feature of recent class analysis has been a convergence in viewpoint between mainstream empirical sociological researchers and the 'post-Marxist' discourse approaches concerning the rejection of orthodox structural Marxist accounts of the relation between class position and consciousness. Central to this convergence are a series of arguments concerning the importance of 'non-class' identities or subject-positions in theorizing contemporary political behaviour.[21]

This is to say that a series of determinations of social agency are conceived as external to the category of class in so far as they cannot be explained as the effects of a necessity given in the logic of economic production; but this in turn means that the category of class is being *reserved* for the realm of that necessity.

Thus—in a passage that I quoted in the previous chapter—Chantal Mouffe sets up as follows the reasons for the virtual irrelevance of the concept of class within the move that she and Ernesto Laclau make to disarticulate discursive domains from each other: use of the concept, she says, opens up one of two options:

We can use the concept of class to designate positions at the level of the relations of production, but in that case we cannot deduce from it anything necessary concerning politics or ideology. Or, we can reserve the term to designate collectivities in struggle at the political level and whose objectives include the transformation of the relations of production. But in this case we cannot know anything

---

[21] Janeen Baxter, Michael Emmison, John Western, *Class Analysis and Contemporary Australia* (Melbourne: Macmillan, 1991), 11.

necessary concerning the position of those agents in the process of production.[22]

As a consequence, she concludes, 'the concept of hegemony is more fundamental than class, since the role that the class positionality plays in the constitution of political subjects depends on the type of hegemony existing in society at a given moment'.[23]

This is a hegemony defined neither in terms of a hegemonic class nor of the interests yielded by such a class's relation to the relations of production; and the aporia to which this thesis inevitably leads is that, if there are no necessary effects of an agent's place in production, or if there are no determinate connections between the distinct domains of discursive positioning, including the economic, then it becomes impossible to construct a coherently relational account of social interests. As Tony Bennett argues, if we except Laclau and Mouffe's appeal to 'left-' and 'right-wing' positionalities, since these are purely contextual terms and have no self-evidence, then there is 'no logical reason why, from Laclau and Mouffe's perspective, the struggle of workers versus capitalists should be politically privileged above, or regarded as more left-wing than, the anti-statist arguments of small businessmen—arguments which often claim precisely the radical democratic political lineage upon which Laclau and Mouffe seek to found a new political imaginary'.[24]

The move made by Laclau and Mouffe to disarticulate the domains of the social, and indeed to refuse any totalized notion of the social system, is similar to that made within a more generalized post-Marxist discourse. Paul Hirst's significantly entitled essay 'Economic Classes and Politics', for example, sets up a conceptual opposition between 'classes of economic agents' and 'political institutions, practices and ideologies', in order then to refuse any causal linkage between them in so far as classes 'are not directly present' and are not

---

[22] Laclau and Mouffe, 'Recasting Marxism', 107–8.
[23] Ibid. 108.
[24] Tony Bennett, *Outside Literature* (London: Routledge, 1990), 266.

visible as social actors in day-to-day political struggles.[25] Political interests are formed specifically by and within the political apparatus, rather than being transposed to it from some other domain. Thus not only is there no necessary correspondence between political institutions and 'economic classes', there is a *necessary non-correspondence* between them.[26]

The central argument here, as also in Barry Hindess's *Politics and Class Analysis*,[27] is that, given the specificity of political forces (political parties, trade unions, pressure groups, and so on) and the impossibility of deriving them directly from or reducing them logically to social classes, which in any case are complex in themselves and complicated by their relation to other structures such as gender and race, there is therefore *no* connection to be found between 'economic class' and the forces operating in the political arena, and certainly classes themselves are not such forces. All this depends, however, on understanding classes as 'economic', and on a refusal to conceive social forces in terms of a multiple and dispersed causality (since either there is a fully determinant 'last instance' or, apparently, there is pure indeterminacy). Cutting the tie between class and politics, both Hirst and Hindess continue to assume a motivation for political action—but it is unclear how motives or interests are generated if they are purely internal to the political domain. At the same time, the complex dynamic of social relations of production is relegated to a self-contained sphere of 'the economic' where these relations contaminate nothing else, have effects on no other spheres of life.

But the basic premiss is as false here as it was in Second International Marxism: as Connell bluntly says, there are no such things as 'economic classes'.[28]

---

[25] Paul Hirst, 'Economic Classes and Politics', in Alan Hunt (ed.), *Class and Class Structure* (London: Lawrence and Wishart, 1977), 125.

[26] Ibid. 130.

[27] Barry Hindess, *Politics and Class Analysis* (Oxford: Basil Blackwell, 1987).

[28] R. W. Connell, *Which Way is Up? Essays on Class, Sex and Culture* (Sydney: Allen and Unwin, 1983), 229.

The consequence of throwing out the category of class together with the logic of economism has not been to institute a new and more adequate model of analysis, but to abandon the field to the wilderness of stratification theory, for which, in Don Aitkin's terms, class 'is a concept of merely nominal value: it is simply the term used to subsume the manifold differences in occupation, income, prestige, residence, life-style and education that characterize a complex urban industrial society'.[29] The implication of such a model is that these dimensions are quite disconnected from each other: that they are aggregated rather than structured, or that they form a continuous, indeterminate, and potentially infinite scale without structural polarizations, and therefore without any way of explaining consolidations of discrepant interests.[30] The very act of *listing* the 'factors' that make up social positionalities (age + gender + race + sexual orientation + . . .) assumes, as Judith Butler puts it, 'their discrete, sequential coexistence along a horizontal axis that does not describe their convergences within a social field'.[31]

I am not of course advocating a return to more traditional Marxist models, or to some combination of Marxist and Weberian schemata which would allow the integration of economic with non-economic determinations. All such approaches continue to be organized around the opposition of two logical planes: a deep structure carrying the necessary logic of the economic, and a surface structure where contingent variations on this necessity are played out. As I have suggested, even a move to abandon the level of deep structure continues to depend upon this binary logic as long

[29] Don Aitkin, *Stability and Change in Australian Politics*, 2nd edn. (Canberra: ANU Press, 1982), 130; cited in Baxter *et al.*, *Class Analysis and Contemporary Australia*, 307.

[30] For a fuller account of the inadequacies of stratificationist theory, cf. Karel Kosík, *Die Dialektik des Konkreten: Eine Studie zur Problematik des Menschen und der Welt*, trans. Marianne Hoffmann (Frankfurt am Main: Suhrkamp, 1967), 111–13; Anthony Giddens, *The Class Structure of the Advanced Societies* (New York: Harper and Row, 1973), 72–80; Connell, *Which Way is Up?*, 85–97; Wright, *Classes*, 34–7.

[31] Butler, *Gender Trouble*, 13.

as the category of class is understood to be the province of strictly economic determinations.

In building an alternative account I shall draw, with some diffidence, on a central concept in the work of Nicos Poulantzas; and with somewhat more confidence on the work of Adam Przeworski. Let me concede immediately that Poulantzas's work on class is severely flawed by his retention of the category of 'determination in the last instance by the economic', which in practice invalidates the formative roles he assigns to political and cultural struggle; what I draw from his theoretical model, however, is the argument that class is defined not on the terrain of the economic but on each of the levels of economic, political, and ideological structure. Class is the complex effect of these three structural levels, which are the loci at once of determination and of struggle.

The following passage gives one of the central formulations of the argument:

It must be emphasized that ideological and political relations . . . are themselves part of the structural determination of class: there is no question of objective place being the result only of economic place within the relations of production, while political and ideological elements belong simply to class positions. We are not faced, as an old error would have it, on the one hand with an economic 'structure' that alone defines class places, and on the other hand with a class struggle extending to the political and ideological domain. This error today often takes the form of a distinction between '(economic) class situation' on the one hand, and politico-ideological class position on the other. From the start structural class determination involves economic, political and ideological class struggle, and these struggles are all expressed in the form of class positions in the conjuncture.[32]

In order to develop what I take to be potentially fruitful in Poulantzas's work, let me supplement it with a further argument of Adam Przeworski's. Rather than seeing economic relations as having the status of objective conditions and all other relations as 'subjective' or contingent,

[32] Nicos Poulantzas, *Classes in Contemporary Capitalism*, trans. David Fernbach (London: Verso, 1975), 16.

Przeworski elaborates a model of class 'in which economic, political, and ideological conditions jointly structure the realm of struggles that have as their effect the organization, disorganization, or reorganization of classes. Classes must thus be viewed as effects of struggles structured by objective conditions that are simultaneously economic, political, and ideological'—and that have indeterminate outcomes.[33] Classes are thus not the direct effects of structure but the outcome, never given in advance, of struggles which take place at all three structural levels.

This seems to me to introduce the measure of indeterminacy that post-Marxist theorists like Laclau seek, without surrendering the structuring moment of objective conditions. Thus, as Przeworski argues, whereas the traditional formulation of class struggles 'either reduces them to an epiphenomenon or enjoins them with freedom from objective determination', this model posits that 'classes are not given uniquely by any objective positions because they constitute effects of struggles, and these struggles are not determined uniquely by the relations of production'.[34] They 'are not a datum prior to the history of concrete struggles';[35] and ideological and political struggles constitute a process, not of class-*representation* (that is, representation of pre-given interests) but of class-*formation* (including the formation of class interests).

This takes me to the core of my argument. Let me articulate it in terms of a number of theses:

1. Class is not an economic structure with effects on other dimensions; class structure is defined in each of the economic, the political, and the ideological spheres.

2. There is no necessary congruence or homology between these spheres: it is precisely *because* of this that we can take

[33] Przeworski, *Capitalism and Social Democracy*, 47 (this passage was initially published in 'Proletariat into a Class: The Process of Class Formation from Karl Kautsky's *The Class Struggle* to Recent Controversies', *Politics and Society*, 7: 4 (1977), 343).

[34] Ibid. 66–7.

[35] Ibid. 69.

political action or rational arguments (and indeed irrational arguments) seriously, as not being reducible to economic position and to an 'interest' defined elsewhere.

3. Class position is thus not necessarily unified or non-contradictory.

4. Each of the three structural spheres is an arena of struggle and of class-formation—not of fixed class positions. Class interests exist not as 'underlying' or objective relations or outcomes but as hypotheses, more or less rationally calculated (or miscalculated). There is no objective criterion of interest given by history or by a non-class or supra-class knowledge: every assessment of interest is itself interested.

5. Since each sphere is a domain of struggle, each is therefore organized as a bundle of economic, political, and ideological relations which constitute its material conditions of existence.

In what follows I try to spell out some of the implications of this final thesis, which produces a considerably more complex map of the structural conditions of class formation.

In diagrammatic form, the more complex map of the conditions of class formation that I propose would look something like this:

	sphere of production	political sphere	ideological sphere
economic class relations	ownership of the means of production (economic capital); the technical division of labour	distribution of political capital within government, political institutions, and the family	possession of symbolic capital (formal or informal qualifications, recognition of social legitimacy)
political class relations	relations of struggle and control in and over the work process ('organization assets') on the basis of legal relations securing property rights	relations of fealty and/or solidarity within kinship and affinity groups, and capacities for struggle with other groups	antagonistically structured status relations ('distinction') and symbolizations of group adherence
ideological class relations	distinction between manual and mental labour ('skill assets'); relations of gender, race, ethnicity	political belief systems, codes of obligation and loyalty, shared narratives of struggle	semiotic constructions of the subject form; the sense of self-identity and identifications of the social Other

Several explanatory codas need to be added to clarify this diagram:

a. This map does not describe or predict what classes there are. It specifies the range of areas in which class struggle, and therefore the experience of belonging to a class, take place. It does not specify the weight to be given to these areas, since this weighting is always a matter of particular historical circumstance.

b. Actual experiences and assignments of class would be the result of a more complex version of the map in which each area would be subject to historically and geographically specific binarizations (of the form +/- possession of economic capital, for example, or +/- membership of a dominant religious group). Any operationalization of the schema would similarly have to convert it into a complex and locally sensitive scoring system with a binary structure—with the degree of complexity or delicacy determined by the requirements of the analysis.

c. Rather than positing a relation between economic *production* and political and ideological *reproduction*, the model suggests that processes of reproduction of social relations, as well as failures and contestations of reproduction, are aspects of each sphere. Similarly, despite the heuristic distinction, all social relations are made up of elements that are *simultaneously* economic, political, and ideological.

d. Relations *between* the three spheres, and between sets of relations of struggle within each sphere, are relatively contingent; there is no necessary coherence or overlap between positionings in each sphere, and the *experience* of class may be discrepant in each.

e. The inclusion of gender, race, and ethnicity as an 'ideological' moment within the domain of production is not intended to indicate that these categories are somehow illusory, but on the contrary to indicate the way in which ideological values attributed to gender, race, and ethnicity work to structure relations of production.

f. Thus the category of gender, for example, must be taken as an overdetermining aspect of every area of class relations. Within the production process it operates to organize the division of labour by determining what counts and what doesn't count as a skill, and then to assign valued skills to men and devalued skills to women.[36] It organizes separate status hierarchies for men and women, it allocates gender-differential positions within kinship systems, and it supports the richly consequential distinction between the private and the public domains. In the same way, class is always, and to a greater or lesser extent, at once overdetermined by and overdeterminant of ethnicity. The particular articulation of class and ethnicity is always nationally and regionally specific, but seems in many cases to have greater force in relation to the working class than to the more nationally unified middle and upper classes. Ethnic rivalry is one of the most common forms taken by class struggle and class hatred (both between classes and within a class). In the United States, to be of Polish or Italian, Irish or Jewish, Puerto Rican or African-American descent is to have alternative modes of access to and integration in class, at the same time as ethnic identity is always rigorously positioned *within* a racially structured class hierarchy, the crucial fact about which is that it is the class of former slaves, not the (white) working class, which occupies the bottom rung.[37] In Australia, working-class identity is fatefully intertwined with Irishness and Roman Catholicism, even where these are purely virtual inheritances.

g. Like race and ethnicity under some historical circumstances, gender is in all societies so crucial a determinant of class relations that it must be asked whether it is theoretically adequate simply to integrate it as a sub-system of class. My

[36] Cf. Ann Game and Rosemary Pringle, *Gender at Work* (Sydney: Allen and Unwin, 1983), 19.

[37] On the interconnections of class, race, and ethnic identity in the United States, cf. Richard D'Alba, *Ethnic Identity: The Transformation of White America* (New Haven, Conn: Yale University Press, 1990); David D. Roediger, *The Wages of Whiteness: Race and the Making of the American Working Class* (London: Verso, 1991).

tentative preference is to use two different modes of description, according to the task at hand. The first speaks of a class–gender system as a way of talking about specific local relations where the two are methodologically inseparable. The second speaks of gender as a separate system that is inevitably enmeshed in the class system; the latter strategy will be used wherever class relations are not the primary focus of the analysis, or where it becomes important to decentre the concept of class in order to stress that it should not work as a totalizing category.[38] The centrality of class to various forms of social explanation is no more than an explanatory convenience; the category will in its turn show up as a *sub*system in accounts that are concerned primarily with the system of gender or of race or of age. Social interpretation deals with multiple centres (or with no centre) and can only ever account for a heuristic confluence of factors for a particular explanatory purpose.

h. To take this a little further: what is it that makes this a *class* map rather than simply a map of general social determinations? Shouldn't the concept of class be tied above all to the social relations of production, and isn't this perhaps a reason for reintroducing a notion of the primacy of or the structural overdetermination of other spheres by the economic? My answer is that any such notion inevitably leads to the negation of the specificity of political and cultural processes. What makes this a class map is the decision to read it that way: that is, the decision to read it in terms of a possible or actual linkage, however indirect or discontinuous, between the three spheres, giving rise to historical consolidations of interests. Other social maps (those of gender or ethnicity, for example) will privilege other kinds of linkage, though they may contain many of the same features.

[38] One of the most lucid discussions of the distinction between the systems of class and gender remains Gayle Rubin, 'The Traffic in Women: Notes on the "Political Economy" of Sex', in Rayner R. Reiter (ed.), *Toward an Anthropology of Women* (New York and London: Monthly Review Press, 1975); cf. also Annette Kuhn and AnnMarie Wolpe, 'Introduction', *Feminism and Materialism: Women and Modes of Production* (London: Routledge and Kegan Paul, 1978), 8.

i. This is perhaps the point at which to indicate how I think it is possible to use the category of class in a non-systemic way. Clearly the full map of class determinants is both impossibly cumbersome and complex, and impossibly totalizing in its scope. It can however in practice always be replaced by a shorthand citation of the analytical features relevant to a particular situation or a particular argument, and these would be hybrid in form (class/gender, class/race, class/kinship). Rather than being a catalogue or a proliferating taxonomy, the use of the map would be pragmatic in its orientation and responsive both to the complex hybridity and fluidity of all actual social positions and to the *limits* of class explanation. There is no internal necessity for it to function as a totalizing concept.

j. The force of Poulantzas's characterization of the distinction between manual and mental labour as *ideological* is that it allows him to specify the domain of production as constituted by processes of political and cultural struggle. The distinction, he writes, is 'directly bound up with the monopolization of knowledge' and correspondingly with 'the permanent exclusion on the subordinated side of those who are deemed not to "know how"'.[39] The distinction works irrespective of whether the 'direct producers' possess a knowledge or a competence which they are not in a position to use, or do not possess it because it has been kept from them, or indeed of whether there is nothing that needs to be known. It is a relational—which is to say a politically constructed—distinction, since the fact is that 'every kind of work includes "mental activity", but . . . not every kind of work is located on the mental labour side in the politico-ideological division between mental and manual labour'.[40] And it is based in a schooling system the primary function of which 'is not to "qualify" manual and mental labour in different ways, but far more to disqualify manual labour', and which works through 'the inculcation of a series of rituals,

[39] Poulantzas, *Classes in Contemporary Capitalism*, 237.
[40] Ibid. 254.

secrets and symbolisms which are to a considerable extent those of "general culture", and whose main purpose is to distinguish [mental labour] from manual labour'.[41] This dimension, then, will constitute a key criterion in the definition of the class of intellectuals.

k. Finally, the model makes it possible to dispense with the notion of objectively pre-given class interests, and to avoid the aporia of what happens when a class turns out not to be *interested* in its supposedly real interests: the classic dilemma of revolutionary Marxism. If class formation is based on struggle in three dimensions, then interests are constituted by and within (and—crucially—*between*) the economic, the political, and the symbolic institutions of this formation. It is a question of the discursive *representation* of interests, of calculation and hypothesis. There is no class essence and there are no unified class actors, founded in the objectivity of a social interest; there are, however, processes of class formation, without absolute origin or telos, with definite discursive conditions, and played out through particular institutional forms and balances of power, through calculations and miscalculations, through desires, and fears, and fantasies.

Most dispute in recent class theory has had to do with the relations *between* the areas mapped by this sketch of the conditions of class formation, and with the positional inconsistencies and discontinuities they produce. Theories of class structure have thus had to devise means either of resolving or of accepting the ambiguity of certain key class positions. Central amongst these has been that class (the stratum of 'intellectuals' in the broadest sense of the word) whose existence is grounded in the possession and exercise of knowledge. In returning to the question of the common interests of this group, let me briefly mention four influential and roughly coincidental accounts: that given by Gouldner

---

[41] Poulantzas, *Classes in Contemporary Capitalism*, 268.

(amongst others)[42] of a so-called New Class of intellectuals and the technical intelligentsia; the Ehrenreichs' concept of a professional-managerial class; the account by Offe, Goldthorpe, Urry, and others of a service class; and Wright's various descriptions of the class of semi-autonomous employees, occupying a contradictory class location.

Methodologically, all four can be read as a response to the major dilemma of recent Marxist class theory: the question of how to take seriously the existence of substantial middle-class groupings in advanced capitalism without either reducing them to one of the 'fundamental' classes (as in the 'new working class' theory of Gorz and Mallet)[43] or characterizing them as a 'residual' class within a two-class framework (Poulantzas's account of the 'new petty-bourgeoisie').[44] There is disagreement, however, on the extent to which these groupings comprise a distinct and more or less homogeneous class.

Alvin Gouldner has the longest historical view of the emergence of such a class, locating its origins in the Enlightenment processes of secularization and modernization, in the culture of rationality and personal autonomy that emerges from the localized, ascriptive, interdependent culture of feudalism, and, above all, in the institution of public education (and, one might add, in the formation of markets in which educational qualifications are exchangeable values).[45] Its importance as a force in developed capitalism is due,

---

[42] Gouldner draws upon the work of Djilas and of Szelenyi and Konrad on the formation of a 'new class' of intellectuals and functionaries in the former communist bloc; Milovan Djilas, *The New Class: An Analysis of the Communist System* (New York: Praeger, 1957); Gyorgy Konrad and Ivan Szelenyi, *The Intellectuals on the Road to Class Power*, trans. Andrew Arato and Richard C. Allen (Brighton: Harvester, 1978).

[43] André Gorz, *Farewell to the Working Class: An Essay on Post-Industrial Socialism*, trans. Michael Sonenscher (Boston: South End Press, 1982); Serge Mallet, *La Nouvelle classe ouvrière* (Paris: Seuil, 1963).

[44] Poulantzas, *Classes in Contemporary Capitalism*.

[45] Alvin W. Gouldner, *The Future of Intellectuals and the Rise of the New Class: A Frame of Reference, Theses, Conjectures, Arguments, and an Historical Perspective on the Role of Intellectuals and Intelligentsia in the International Class Contest of the Modern Era* (New York: Oxford University Press, 1979), 1; further citations are given in the text.

however, to a number of structural changes. Wright identifies these as follows: 'the progressive loss of control over the labour process on the part of the direct producers; the elaboration of complex authority hierarchies within capitalist enterprises and bureaucracies; and the differentiation of various functions originally embodied in the entrepreneurial capitalist'.[46]

The developing autonomy of managerial functions is bound up with two great movements that stretch across most of the twentieth century: the increasingly specialized role of managers in the conception and design of labour processes, and the tendential separation of financial and legal *ownership* from the effective *possession* and control of large (public or private) corporations.[47] In its relation to the work process, then, this professional-managerial class has developed its powers by successfully laying claim to sole possession of expertise in crucial areas and at the expense of the skills and knowledges possessed both by workers and by the owners of enterprises.

But the claim to a monopoly of knowledges extends beyond the process of material production. In the terms used by the Ehrenreichs, the social function of this class is in the broadest sense the reproduction of the class structure of capitalism (and indeed, Gouldner would add, of state capitalism). The concept of reproduction, however, works in several rather different senses: minimally, it means both the ongoing reorganization of the productive process through scientific and managerial innovation, and the reproduction of social relations through the schooling system and the culture industries. In both cases it involves a use of knowledge, but of rather different kinds.[48]

---

[46] Erik Olin Wright, *Class, Crisis and the State* (London: Verso, 1979), 64.

[47] The thesis of an increasing separation of ownership and control was articulated as early as 1941 in James Burnham's *The Managerial Revolution: What is Happening in the World?* (New York: John Day, 1941). For a critique of the argument, cf. Maurice Zeitlin, 'Corporate Ownership and Control: The Large Corporation and the Capitalist Class', in Anthony Giddens and David Held (eds.), *Classes, Power, and Conflict: Classical and Contemporary Debates* (London: Macmillan, 1982), 196–223.

[48] Barbara and John Ehrenreich, 'The Professional-Managerial Class', in Pat Walker (ed.), *Between Labor and Capital* (Boston: South End Press, 1979), 12.

It is this difference that provokes—quite fundamentally for all four groups of theorists—the question of the coherence of a class which is by definition larger than its managerial or technocratic wing. What might subtend its unity as a whole? Gouldner gives two complementary answers to this question. The first is situated at the infrastructural level: the unity of the New Class derives from its possession of cultural capital, a term that, far from being merely a metaphor, designates a real stock which, like a stock of money capital, generates privately appropriated income.[49] The second is cultural: the New Class is bonded as a class by its formation as a speech community characterized by 'an orientation to a qualitatively special culture of speech: to the culture of careful and critical discourse' (p. 27). By this Gouldner means something like a discursive ethos: such a culture relies on justification by argument rather than by an appeal to authority or precedent; like Bernstein's elaborated code, it values explicitness and universality of reference; above all, it is inherently self-reflexive and self-problematizing (pp. 27–9). As enlightened reason it thus underlies both technical or instrumental reason and critical or symbolic reason—and is thus at some level common both to 'intellectuals' and to the 'technical intelligentsia'.

[49] I have no strong position on the question of whether or not the term 'cultural capital'—like the term 'human capital', with which it is historically connected—is a metaphor, since I am not convinced that the question is well posed. The Swedish sociologist Adam Westoby puts forward the following arguments that it should be treated as a metaphor: 'Knowledge, as intangible and universal, can only give rise to stretched and imperfect property rights. It cannot assume a full commodity form, and its circulation and expansion cannot rest fundamentally on exchange. New theoretical knowledge, for example, supplants and modifies the existing stock directly, not through devaluing it. And as far as the structures of motivation facing the individual "capital" are concerned, any similarities are superficial: to the essentially quantitative, unbounded expansion of money capital corresponds the qualitative and finite life, education, and career of the individual.' Westoby, 'Mental Work, Education, and the Division of Labour', 148–9. This presupposes, however, that there exists a literal or fundamental form of capital (money, for example); I disagree. Capital is a purely relational concept, the most abstract and disembodied of all economic concepts. It is a historically specific social *relation*, involving commodity production, private ownership of the means of production, and the objectification of labour power; and in all these respects it seems to me that it can take the form of socialized knowledge as well as it can that of, for example, money capital.

For reasons that I shall try to explain later, the key arguments for the unity of a knowledge class tend to be made in terms of its culture of work, rather than in terms of the similarity of the work performed. Let me isolate three dimensions of this 'cultural' explanation of class cohesion.

The first has to do with a set of common institutions and processes of socialization. As the Ehrenreichs argue, the professional-managerial class is knit together by a culture which includes distinctive patterns of family life, a shared ideology of social rationalization, and specific institutions of socialization (those of tertiary education). The university and the professional body, and the claim to specialized knowledge which they embody, are what enables the professional-managerial class to control its own reproduction. This is perhaps the most insightful aspect of their discussion: the recognition of the importance for this class of the reproduction of positions which, rather than being inherited, are acquired only within the class-*productive* apparatus of education. Hence the importance of control of this sphere.[50]

The second dimension concerns more specifically the culture and organization of work. In its relation to the ruling class the knowledge class is caught uneasily between its real subordination in the service of capital and its ethos of independence. This ethos has a grounding in the relatively high degree of autonomy characterizing its work practices, and in the organization of its mode of work by the structure of the profession. Professionalism is defined by three kinds of claim: to the possession of a specialized body of knowledge; to the upholding of ethical standards; and to the need for autonomy from outside scrutiny and control. These claims are

[50] Immanuel Wallerstein writes that the new middle class is differentiated from the working class by its possession of 'human capital', which is acquired 'in the educational systems, whose primary and self-proclaimed function is to train people to become members of the new middle classes, that is, to be the professionals, the technicians, the administrators of the private and public enterprises which are the functional economic building-pieces of our system'; thus 'a key locus of political struggle is the rules of the educational game'. 'The Bourgeois(ie) as Concept and Reality', *New Left Review*, 167 (1988), 105.

of course a matter of political struggle, but they also tacitly lay a further claim, to ethical and social enlightenment.

The third dimension of class cohesion is elaborated around the notion of a 'service' class and the particular form of rationality associated with service work. For Claus Offe, service activities are structured by the need to respect both the particularity of the needs of clients and the establishment of a *generalized* state of regularity; the need to achieve a balance between the 'specificity of the case' and the 'generality of the norm'.[51] Service labour is thus caught between the contractual and highly controlled rationality of 'industrial economy', and a more open-ended rationality of mediation and conciliation (p. 107). This emphasis on the structure of employment or the 'code of service' is extended by John Goldthorpe in terms of the ethical structure (the relationship of 'trust') which differentiates service work from the strictly controlled exchanges of the labour contract.[52]

It is around these three dimensions that the claim is made for a commonality of culture that would make it possible, and make it taxonomically illuminating, to group together such disparate occupational groupings as cultural workers, engineers, scientists, managers, and so on. In fact, no one of these four accounts is entirely successful in mapping contemporary class relations in such a way as to produce a coherent and integrated model of the knowledge class and its social interests. But two things need to be said about this. The first is that each of these accounts, though partial and limited, has generated strong insights into the conditions of possibility and the defining characteristics of such a class. The second is that the demand itself—for coherence and integration—may

[51] Claus Offe, *Disorganized Capitalism: Contemporary Transformations of Work and Politics*, ed. John Keane (Cambridge: Polity Press, 1985), 106.

[52] John Goldthorpe, 'On the Service Class, Its Formation and Future', in Anthony Giddens and Gavin Mackenzie (eds.), *Social Class and the Division of Labour: Essays in Honour of Ilya Neustadt* (Cambridge: Cambridge University Press, 1982), 162–85. Goldthorpe's essay draws extensively on Karl Renner's pioneering essay on the *Dienstklasse, Wandlungen der modernen Gesellschaft: Zwei Abhandlungen über die Probleme der Nachkriegzeit* (Vienna: Verlag der Wiener Volksbuchhandlung, 1953).

be wrongly formulated in supposing the objective existence of class structures. Rather than asking 'what classes are there?', or 'who is in this class?', we should perhaps be concerned with class as a theoretical construct with discursive effects. Thus the value of positing the claim to possession of knowledge as a key criterion for defining the knowledge class may be a strategic rather than a descriptive value: it works to *set up* a relation between cultural intellectuals and a broader social grouping which has some shared social interests, a fiction that may or may not prove fruitful.

John Goldthorpe has challenged the usefulness of seeking to define the knowledge class, or service class, 'in terms of their distinctive possession of "cultural capital" or of their "command over theoretical knowledge"',[53] since data on credential levels indicate considerable cross-national variation. But the point here must be that what is at issue is the *claim* to knowledge rather than its actual possession, and that credentials are only one of the ways in which this claim can be pursued. This is the reason why I signalled the importance of Poulantzas's situation of the distinction between manual and mental labour as an *ideological* dimension of the production process. His argument makes it possible to take a good deal further an exploration of some of the crucial determinants of the organization of work and of the social relations bound up with it.

The historical conditions for the growth of a class based in the performance of knowledge functions are, very broadly, these:

First, the protracted development of a public sector in which a range of ethico-disciplinary functions—those of education, of public health, and a variety of welfare services—are removed from the family or the kinship network and assumed as State responsibilities.[54] The

---

[53] Goldthorpe, 'On the Service Class', 174.

[54] The distinction between the public and the private sectors is not in itself the crucial one, since the distribution of services between these sectors varies considerably from country to country, and many 'public' functions may be handled by 'private' agencies; the determinant factor is the autonomization of

constitution of 'the population' as an object of knowledge and of deliberate policy measures is the formative moment in the establishment of this sector.[55]

Second, the transformation and diversification of the managerial functions involved in controlling the work process: on the one hand the development of the techniques and ideologies of 'scientific management', which radically separate the functions of labour and of knowledge; on the other the increased importance to mass industrial production of the co-ordinating functions of contractual regulation, accountancy and financial services, computing, 'human resource' management, and so on.

Third, the growth in complexity of the planning function, including research and development, market research, and advertising. As Abercrombie and Urry point out, it is the reduction in contemporary capitalism of the turnover time of fixed capital that forces the expansion of technological innovation and of the controlled generation of desires, and thus makes these functions central to capitalist production.[56]

Each of these clusters of historical transformations is closely bound up with, and has powerful consequences upon, the tendential separation of 'manual' from 'mental' labour. Their effect, however, is not to produce a dichotomous class structure (workers and capitalists) but to generate new occupational groups with alternative grounds for formation as a class. These grounds include—to summarize briefly—the definition of members as 'mental' workers with specialist expertise; the possession of cultural capital in the form of

these functions: their socialization, and their ultimate regulation by the state. Cf. however the argument made by Harold Perkin in *The Rise of Professional Society: England Since 1880* (London and New York: Routledge, 1989) that 'the struggle between the public and private sector professions is the master conflict of professional society' (p. 10)—by which he means contemporary advanced-capitalist societies, which are dominated in all aspects by the 'professional class'.

[55] Michel Foucault, 'Governmentality', in Graham Burchell, Colin Gordon, and Peter Miller (eds.), *The Foucault Effect: Studies in Governmentality, with Two Lectures by and an Interview with Michel Foucault* (Chicago: University of Chicago Press, 1991).

[56] Nicholas Abercrombie and John Urry, *Capital, Labour and the Middle Classes* (London: Allen and Unwin, 1983), 97.

credentials; the claim to autonomous work conditions; and the enforcement of this claim, as well as the organization of a loose class cohesion, through professional associations or similar forms of peer recognition.

The development of new class relations, however, transforms the existing ones, and in this case transforms, above all, social understandings of what *counts* as knowledge. The ideology of rationalized, 'scientific' management was decisive in this respect in that it defined 'manual' workers as lacking in relevant knowledge. More precisely, by analysing production into its discrete stages and components, and then retraining workers in the mechanical performance of these disconnected and incoherent fragments of a total operation, it acted to strip them of their craft knowledge and to reinvest it in the 'specialist' manager.[57] (The process of appropriation of craft knowledges is taken to its extreme in robotization.) The result of this reorganization of work is not exactly a de-skilling, but rather, as Littek and Heisig argue, the establishment of a hierarchical division between knowledge and skill.[58] Crucially, both knowledge and skill are strongly gendered concepts: definitions of what counts as skilled work tend to exclude work performed by women (both paid and unpaid),[59] and within the domain of 'mental' labour there is a clear hierarchical distinction between routine and non-routine work, again to the disadvantage of women; lower-level clerical, teaching, and white-collar service work are now preponderantly female sectors.

The grounds on which the 'new middle class' of knowledge-workers is formed constitute at the same time the foundations for its social interests and for its 'causal

---

[57] The classic source is still Harry Braverman, *Labor and Monopoly Capital: The Degradation of Work in the Twentieth Century* (New York: Monthly Review Press, 1974).

[58] Wolfgang Littek and Ulrich Heisig, 'Work Organization under Technological Change: Sources of Differentiation and the Reproduction of Social Inequality in Processes of Change', in Stewart R. Clegg (ed.), *Organization Theory and Class Analysis: New Approaches and New Issues* (Berlin and New York: Walter de Gruyter, 1990), 303.

[59] Game and Pringle, *Gender at Work*, 18.

powers'.[60] As these increase, so the powers of the working class, dispossessed of its traditional knowledges, decline. The relation is not, however, one of a simple inverse proportion: the working class is not reduced to being a passive instrument (nor should we idealize a mythical past in which it had full control over the production process); nor is knowledge 'owned' by the professional-managerial middle class. Certainly knowledge, especially economically productive knowledge, can be privately appropriated, and the whole apparatus of intellectual property law exists to sustain this possibility; but ownership is vested in that class which owns the rest of the means of production, not in knowledge workers. Alternatively, knowledge which is in the public domain circulates within the *institutions* of science, the professions and education, rather than being the property of its individual users.[61] The power of the knowledge class is the power of legitimate access to and use of this domain of knowledge, and the power to define what this domain is; but it should not be forgotten that there are other and more decisive powers.[62]

The origins of the knowledge class lie in an expansion and a transformation of the roles of the traditional intelligentsia. One wing derives from the intelligentsia of letters: from the

---

[60] Scott Lash and John Urry define the latter as being: 'to restructure capitalist societies so as to maximize the divorce between conception and execution and to ensure the elaboration of highly differentiated and specific structures within which knowledge and science can be developed and sustained. These powers thus involve the deskilling of productive labourers; the maximizing of the educational requirements of places within the social division of labour and the minimizing of non-educational/non-achievement criteria for recruitment to such places; and the enhancement of the resources and income devoted to education and science (whether this is privately or publicly funded).' Lash and Urry, *The End of Organized Capitalism* (Cambridge: Polity Press, 1987), 177–8; this passage is a slight reworking of a passage in Abercrombie and Urry, *Capital, Labour and the Middle Classes*, 132.

[61] Cf. Lash and Urry, *The End of Organized Capitalism*, 194.

[62] 'The means of mental production—laboratories, universities, television stations—are rarely owned by their workers, and indeed in most of these sectors we have recently seen an increasing assertion of external control, by other capitals and powers than those of pure ideas.' Michael Rustin, 'The Politics of Post-Fordism: Or, the Trouble with "New Times"', *New Left Review*, 175 (May/June 1989), 66.

priest, the teacher, and the journalist, who share between them the tasks of the cure of souls, the propagation of enlightenment, and the inculcation of ruling-class ideology. The other wing derives from the technical intelligentsia, especially the 'old' professions and the somewhat younger profession of engineering, which have as their function the application of useful knowledge. But speaking of origins says nothing of present structures. What, finally, allows us to imagine that this class possesses some integrating principle of unity?

To pose the question in this way is to assume that intellectual workers are held together as a class by a common bond—whether it be that of a common social function, or of a shared experience of class socialization, of a common experience and expectation of work, or of the jointly undertaken risk of investment in cultural rather than monetary capital. The most likely hypothesis, however—since otherwise there would not be so serious a problem of definition—is that it does constitute a more or less coherent class in some respects but not in others; the new middle class (the knowledge class) is an entity that doesn't respond well (for good structural reasons, I think) to the question: is this a fully formed class?[63]

[63] Ralf Dahrendorf gives a lucid orthodox definition of the distinction between class and stratum. Classes, he says, are '"major interest groupings emerging from specific structural circumstances, which intervene as such in social conflicts and play a part in changes of social structure". Whereas a "stratum" is merely an analytical category, identifying persons of a similar situation in the social hierarchy, who share some situational identities such as "income, prestige, style of living, etc."' Ralf Dahrendorf, *Soziale Klassen und Klassenkonflikt* (Stuttgart, 1957), pp. ix, 139; quoted in Alec Nove, 'Is There a Ruling Class in the USSR?', in Anthony Giddens and David Held (eds.), *Classes, Power and Conflict* (London: Macmillan, 1982), 602. Paradoxically, many Marxist theorists resort to stratification theory in order to solve the conceptual untidiness of the middle classes. Thus Alex Callinicos argues that the new middle class is not a 'proper' class with a 'distinct and coherent set of interests deriving [from] their position in the relations of production'; it is no more than 'a collection of heterogeneous social layers who have in common an ambiguous and intermediate position with respect to the fundamental contradiction between capital and wage-labour'. Alex Callinicos, 'The "New Middle Class" and Socialist Politics', *International Socialism*, 2: 20 (1983), 103–4. Since I have no commitment to the model of a fundamental *and unmediated* contradiction, however, the distinction between class and stratum loses much of its importance.

There is, nevertheless, a valid and difficult question to be asked about the composition of the knowledge class. This is not quite the question: 'Who is in this class?' (a question that corresponds to a naïvely realist epistemology), but is rather a question about the consequences of theoretical choices made in describing the make-up of the class, and of the logic according to which these choices should be made. For example: should upper-level managers be said to belong to the knowledge class? The answer will depend not just on how this class itself is conceived but on our conception of the interlocking structure of relations *between* classes, on the particular criteria of class membership that we apply, and on how individuals identify themselves.[64] Wright notes at one point that the consequence of Poulantzas's narrow definition of the working class in terms of productive material labour is that the working class of the United States would constitute less than 20% of the economically active population, and the petty bourgeoisie would constitute some 70%.[65] Burris's schematization (Figure 3) of the different maps of class relations produced by the models of Poulantzas, C. Wright Mills, the Ehrenreichs, Carchedi, and Wright illustrates even more graphically the consequences of theoretical choices (although Burris of course implicitly privileges his own mapping of the class structure in doing so).[66]

There are choices to be made, then, but no objective criteria given in the statistical data or in the self-consciousness of individuals against which to measure their correctness. The

[64] That is, on whether they perceive some sort of commonality of interests and culture with others whom we assign to the class; but note that this perception of salience need not take the form of an articulate sociological definition; and it may involve a *denial* of a particular or indeed of any class status.

[65] Wright, *Class, Crisis and the State*, 55. To say this is not necessarily to make a criticism, as Wright seems to believe.

[66] Note that Burris seems to me to be wrong in assuming that Guglielmo Carchedi assigns managers and supervisors to the new middle class, since Carchedi explicitly differentiates them. On p. 96 of *On the Economic Identification of Social Classes* (London: Routledge, 1977), for example, he writes that 'the top manager has real, economic ownership and thus has economic power. He must delegate a part of his work of control and surveillance to lower managerial strata and to the new middle class.'

Detailed Class Fractions	Poulantzas's Classes	Mills's Classes	Ehrenreichs' Classes	Carchedi's Classes	Wright's Classes
Managers and Supervisors	New Petty Bourgeoisie	New Middle Class	Professional-Managerial Class	New Middle Class	Managers and Supervisors
Professional and Technical Workers					Semi-auton. (credentialled) Employees
Routine Mental Workers			Proletariat	Proletariat	Proletariat
Unproductive Manual Workers		Proletariat			
Productive Manual Workers	Proletariat				

FIG. 3. *Alternative models of class divisions among salaried workers*

Source: Val Burris, 'Class Structure and Political Ideology', *The Insurgent Sociologist*, 14: 2 (Summer 1987), p. 33, fig.1.

criteria, that is to say, can only be those of productiveness and of plausibility—not of descriptive accuracy.

The least problematic structural question concerns, I think, the distinction between the knowledge class and the traditional petty bourgeoisie. The latter own their means of livelihood, may be small employers, and historically have possessed a distinctively illiberal ideology;[67] the overlap with self-employed professionals is therefore not as significant as would be indicated by purely economic criteria.

The division between the knowledge class and the working class is less well-defined, in part because the working class itself is now not so coherent a formation as it was (or as it seems in retrospect to have been) in Fordist capitalism. There is agreement among most theorists that 'routine' white-collar workers—clerical workers, lower public servants, nurses, technicians—are closer to the working class (for example, to skilled tradespeople) than to the credentialled middle classes,

[67] Cf. Frank Bechhofer and Brian Elliott, 'Petty Property: The Survival of a Moral Economy', in Frank Bechhofer and Brian Elliott (eds.), *The Petite Bourgeoisie: Comparative Studies of the Uneasy Stratum* (New York: St Martin's Press, 1981), 182–3.

but the uncertainties of self-definition and particularly the force of class *aspiration* make this boundary ambivalent.[68]

The same is true at the top end of the knowledge class, where upper-level managers, often holding stock in the companies they control or, in the case of public-sector executives, sharing a common managerial culture, merge into the dominant class; similarly, upper-level professionals (for example in the medical and legal professions) pass more or less easily into the *haute bourgeoisie*. The class boundary is thus not an occupational boundary, since it is formed in part by differences that have to do with generation and with class *trajectory* (a notion which is central to understanding the class situation and the calculations of interest of the credentialled middle classes).[69]

The group that remains—professionals, lower- and middle-level managers and administrators, and salaried or self-employed intellectuals, including cultural intellectuals, scientists, and higher-level technicians—is structured 'internally' by multiple splits and antagonisms which I take to be definitive of the class, and which can be grouped in a number of different ways: as a tension between managers and profes-

---

[68] In *Capital, Labour and the Middle Classes*, for example, Nicholas Abercrombie and John Urry differentiate sharply between two groups within what is usually called the 'middle class': de-skilled white-collar workers (lower-grade office and sales employees), on the one hand, and on the other an 'upper' middle class of managers, administrators, and 'established' professionals. This differentiation has a historical dimension: 'With the rationalization of the labour process, the fragmentation and standardization of tasks, and the increasing bureaucratization of administration, the mental labour content of white-collar jobs passes further up the hierarchy. The process of rationalization has undermined the traditional sociological distinction between manual and non-manual work; clerks *are* manual workers.' Abercrombie and Urry, *Capital, Labour and the Middle Classes*, 118.

[69] Cf. Pierre Bourdieu, *Distinction: A Social Critique of the Judgment of Taste*, trans. Richard Nice (Cambridge, Mass.: Harvard University Press, 1984), 110–12; Erik Olin Wright, 'Rethinking, Once Again, the Concept of Class Structure', in Erik Olin Wright *et al.*, *The Debate on Classes* (London: Verso, 1989), 324–34. Alex Callinicos points out that, in contrast to the expectation of sharply rising income for upper white-collar workers, the career trajectory of manual and routine clerical workers is much flatter, rising only in relation to overtime worked and normally declining in later years. Callinicos, 'The "New Middle Class" and Socialist Politics', 103.

sionals; between 'cultural' and 'technical' intellectuals; or between public- and private-sector employees. I call these tensions definitive because it seems to me that the crucial attribute of this class is that it is *weakly formed as a class*. This weakness has to do above all with the fact that the key mechanisms of its formation as a class are those that relate to its claim to knowledge, rather than those that relate to the ownership of the means of production and to direct exploitation.

The formation of the knowledge class characteristically takes place around the professional claim to, and the professional mystique of, autonomy of judgement; this forms the basis both for the struggle over the organization of work and for individual self-respect (that is, for a particular mode of subjectivity) grounded in this relation to work. It underlies the differentiation of middle-class from working-class forms of work: one based in 'knowledge' and structured around loyalty, 'social exchange', and responsibility, the other based in 'skill' and structured around 'low trust, economic exchange and direct control'.[70] At the same time the claim to autonomy underlies the complementary strategies used in the struggle to achieve appropriate working conditions: a professional strategy of arguing that access to specialized mental labour can and should be achieved only by way of institutionally controlled credentials; and a strategy of protecting managerial prerogatives from direct interference by owners.[71] The historical shaping of the knowledge class accordingly took place around a process of legal and industrial struggle over the conditions for autonomy of work practices.[72]

---

[70] Littek and Heisig, 'Work Organization Under Technological Change', 300.

[71] Wright, 'Rethinking, Once Again, the Concept of Class Structure', 339, n. 91.

[72] A number of writers cite the engineering profession in the United States early in the twentieth century as exemplary in its pursuit of an integration of industrial careers with educational credentials—for example, D. Noble, *America by Design* (New York: Oxford University Press, 1979). Lash and Urry write of this process: 'One occupation after another sought to strengthen its market-power by connecting together the production of knowledge with the production of the

The knowledge class acquires legitimacy through the acquisition of credentials, and at the same time achieves a measure of class closure by integrating the community of those with appropriate credentials and excluding those without; it structures its Other in terms of its own claim to knowledge.[73] This closure is then reinforced through the 'cultural' mechanisms of taste and 'lifestyle'.[74] One of the reasons for its relative lack of cohesion as a class, however, is precisely that, as the disciplines of knowledge become institutionalized, it is these *particular* territories of knowledge, and the disciplinary mysteries appropriate to each,[75] rather than knowledge in general, that come to be invested with value. The potential for fractional division that this particularization brings with it is exacerbated by other structural rifts, in particular that between the public sector and the service professions, on the one hand,

producers via the modern university. There was a structural linkage effected between two sets of elements, specific bodies of theoretical knowledge, on the one hand, and markets for skilled services, or labour, on the other. By contrast with, say, nineteenth-century Britain, higher education became the means for bringing about professionalization and for the substantial transformation of the restructuring of social inequality.' (*The End of Organized Capitalism*, 173).

[73] Cf. Randall Collins, *The Credential Society: An Historical Sociology of Education and Stratification* (New York: Academic Press, 1979).

[74] 'Lifestyle' is one of the most obvious defining characteristics of the new middle class; I have paid no attention to the category here because I think its very obviousness can be misleading. Many descriptions of the class—Featherstone's, or Urry's, or Harvey's, for example—use the visibility of lifestyle as the occasion for a moralizing account of the class. Folk-taxonomic terms like 'yuppy' and 'trendy', although they are of considerable interest as indications of popular perceptions of a self-contained class, tend to work the same way. Mike Featherstone, *Consumer Culture and Postmodernism* (London: Sage, 1991), 45–6; John Urry, *The Tourist Gaze: Leisure and Travel in Contemporary Societies* (London: Sage, 1990), 92–3; David Harvey, *The Condition of Postmodernity* (Oxford: Basil Blackwell, 1989), 347–8; Paul Lyons, 'Yuppie: A Contemporary American Keyword', *Socialist Review*, 19: 1 (1989), 111–22.

[75] H. Jamous and B. Peloille distinguish between technical competence over an explicit and testable body of knowledge ('technicality'), and a charismatic mode of *ascribed* knowledge which forms any profession's 'mystery' and which, since it is never codified, cannot be appropriated by outsiders ('indetermination'); the acquisition of credentials for a profession involves in part the acquisition of the 'margin of indetermination' proper to it, which is not transmitted by explicit procedures of training and evaluation. H. Jamous and B. Peloille, 'Changes in the French University-Hospital System', in J. A. Jackson (ed.), *Professions and Professionalization*, Sociological Studies, 3 (Cambridge: Cambridge University Press, 1970), 112, 115.

whose relation to the exploitation of the working class is tangential, and on the other private-sector managers and administrators, who participate directly in exploitation, albeit from the ambivalent position of salaried supervisors.[76] (At the same time, the possibility of critical intellectual work—work that cuts against class attachments—is given, in the *first* instance, not as a matter of ethical decision but in the double fracture that separates the knowledge class from the dominant class and then divides it internally along a number of different fault lines.)

One of Erik Olin Wright's major self-criticisms, however, is that possession of skill assets (knowledge) does not *in itself* constitute an exploitative relation to those without them.[77] If we accept this argument, then it is clear that the knowledge class cannot be defined directly on the axis of exploitation. It is structured by the indirectness of its insertion in the relations of production; by the salience for the way it defines itself of an ideology of autonomous work practice; and by its weak classificatory structure—the fuzziness of its boundaries with other classes.[78] It is a class which is necessarily-not-for-itself, and a class which is coherent only in its lack of structural cohesion. Concomitantly, its interests in the political sphere, reflecting this internal dividedness, are structured by its ambivalently tutelary and antagonistic relation to the working class, its identification with both public and private sectors, and its ethos of professional autonomy and service. Above all, it is formed politically by its close relation to bureaucracy (in both sectors) and to 'flexible' forms of bureaucratic rationality—and thereby to the forms of governmentality most characteristic of advanced capitalism.

'Cultural' factors, including a distinctive culture of work and the career-building role of cultural capital, play a major part in forming the knowledge class as a more or less cohesive

[76] Burris, 'Class Structure and Political Ideology', 39.
[77] Wright, 'Rethinking, Once Again, the Concept of Class Structure', 308–9.
[78] Urry, *The Tourist Gaze*, 88.

group. To make this argument is not, however, to posit a necessary or an expressive relation between class and culture: it is not to assume that this class possesses its own distinctive culture which gives 'expressive form' to its 'social and material life-experience'[79] or endows it with the consciousness of its own historicity.[80] Such assumptions, as I have argued earlier, fail to come to terms with the complexity of 'mass' audience structures, and ignore the crucial mediating role of cultural institutions.

The work that can be done by the category of class, and by specific class analysis, is at once more modest and more negative than this. On the one hand, class analysis can give a sense of the structural limits set to action and desire; on the other, it can act as a check against claims made by members of one social group to an identity of interests with another. I take up this question in the final chapter through an examination of the right claimed by intellectuals to speak on behalf of others. Here let me mention more specifically a concept that has been of central importance to the development of cultural studies, that of the organic intellectual.

In a widely cited passage in the anthology *Cultural Studies* Stuart Hall wrote:

The problem about the concept of an organic intellectual is that it appears to align intellectuals with an emerging historic movement and we couldn't tell then, and can hardly tell now, where that emerging historical movement was to be found. We were organic

[79] Fred Pfeil, 'Makin' Flippy-Floppy: Postmodernism and the Baby-Boom PMC', *Another Tale to Tell: Politics and Narrative in Postmodern Culture* (London: Verso, 1990), 98.

[80] Christa Bürger, 'The Disappearance of Art: The Postmodernism Debate in the US', *Telos*, 68 (1986), 96. Both Pfeil and Bürger are referring to postmodernism as the culture 'of' the new middle class. Cf. Lash and Urry's similar but slightly more cautious claim that 'it is the developing service class which is the consumer *par excellence* of post-modern cultural products; that there is a certain "hegemonizing mission" of the post-modern tastes and lifestyle of significant sections of this new middle class; and that there are certain structural conditions of the service class that produce a decentred identity which fosters the reception of such post-modern cultural goods'. Lash and Urry, *The End of Organized Capitalism*, 292; cf. also Scott Lash, *Sociology of Postmodernism* (London: Routledge, 1990), 20.

intellectuals without any organic point of reference; organic intellectuals with a nostalgia or will or hope (to use Gramsci's phrase from another context) that at some point we would be prepared in intellectual work for that kind of relationship, if such a conjuncture ever appeared. More truthfully, we were prepared to imagine or model or simulate such a relationship in its absence: 'pessimism of the intellect, optimism of the will'.[81]

The problem Hall maps out is that of an intelligentsia 'organically' linked to a class or a historic bloc which has yet to come into being. The sheer virtuality of that link—its existence as 'nostalgia or will or hope'—shoots through with irony the notion that attachment to another class or bloc is the right and proper way for intellectuals to work. Hall reads this failure of attachment in essentially negative terms (as loss or lack); but the metaphors of projection—'imagine or model or simulate'—perhaps suggest another and more positive function of this imaginary relationship. In this alternative reading we might propose that it is a question not of preparation or anticipation but of work conducted in its own time, work with its own impetus and its own historic goals; we might propose, that is to say, that work in cultural studies could be taken seriously in relation to the specific interests of the class of intellectuals rather than in relation to a non-existent historic bloc. But this is perhaps also to say that this work, with its entirely fruitful impetus to explore non-traditional and previously unvalued cultures, was predicated on a necessary blindness to its own class provenance.

Michael Rustin makes a parallel and, I think, persuasive argument about the class bases for the conceptualization of post-Fordism, as it was elaborated by, amongst others, Stuart Hall in a series of 'New Times' articles. The world of flexible specialization, Rustin writes, 'is the world as seen from the point of view of some of its beneficiaries—themselves "flexible specialists" such as researchers, communicators, information

---

[81] Stuart Hall, 'Cultural Studies and its Theoretical Legacies', in Lawrence Grossberg, Cary Nelson, and Paula Treichler (eds.), *Cultural Studies* (New York: Routledge, 1992), 281.

professionals and designers, whose specific capabilities involve the handling and processing of information'.[82] The way in which a particular set of class interests is carried is most evident 'in the high programmatic priority given to education, training and research as functional for "progressive modernization", but also, of course, as central to the life-world of the man or woman for whom the capacity to acquire, apply and transmit knowledge is *the* market resource'.

Correspondingly, even the more 'progressive' aspects of the concept translate interests that are not universal:

arguments for the decentralization of decision-making, for the informal welfare sector, for neighbourhood control, parent power and cooperative housing, also reflect the central position that this new and enlarged intelligentsia is likely to occupy in more pluralized and devolved systems, as the strata who have the cultural capacities to make use of such spaces to find fulfilling and influential roles.[83]

In much the same way, work in cultural studies seems to me to carry both the one interest that can be attributed with some certainty to the knowledge class: a commitment to the institutions of cultural capital, and simultaneously a set of anxieties about its place within these institutions. Displaced from the position of cultural authority which it once believed itself to hold, controlling one rather small market within a pluralized market system, and properly uncertain of its right to speak in and for other cultural domains, the cultural intelligentsia (and most of the knowledge class has some claim to cultural expertise) has been able to construct its own historicity only in the endless deferral of its self-recognition.

[82] Rustin, 'The Politics of Post-Fordism', 63.
[83] Ibid. 64.

4

Economies of Value

> The privileging of the self through the pathologizing of
> the Other remains the key move and defining objective
> of axiology.[1]

From this point onwards I address you, my silent reader,
explicitly as a cultural intellectual: an address which may go
astray, but which enables me to abandon that pretence of
universality—the pretence of the absence of position—which
lends such a false glow of transparency to academic writing. I
assume, for the sake of argument, that when I say 'we' from
now on I am speaking to and partly for men and women
belonging to a local fraction of the class that I have tried to
describe in the previous chapter; I assume that 'we' have
certain—but by no means all—class-specific interests in
common; and that these have to do above all with the
investments we have made in knowledge and its social
relations. I assume you share my uncertainties about the
value of our knowledge and about—the topic of this final
chapter—the positions that we are able to occupy within the
field of cultural value.

I argued earlier that it is no longer either possible or useful
to understand cultural production in terms of a general
economy of value, and thus that we can no longer imagine
ourselves into a vantage point from which conflicting
judgements of value could be reconciled. What may in some
sense always have been the case has become self-evidently so
now: that different social groups employ criteria of value
which may well be incompatible and irreconcilable. Lotman's

[1] Barbara Herrnstein Smith, *Contingencies of Value: Alternative Perspectives
for Critical Theory* (Cambridge, Mass.: Harvard University Press, 1988), 38.

distinction between the aesthetic of opposition that organizes post-Romantic high culture, and the aesthetic of repetition that organizes much of folk and popular culture is perhaps the simplest way of exemplifying this incompatibility; but in general the disjunctions between the organizing aesthetics of European and non-European cultures, between 'men's' and 'women's' genres (in so far as this opposition can be sustained), between religious and 'aesthetic' functionalizations of a text, between literate and oral cultures, between the cultural norms of different age-classes or different sexual subcultures or different national regions, and so on, can be taken as indications of a vastly more complex network of differentiations which is not, or is no longer, reducible to a single scale.

Yet it is precisely this assumption of a set of uniform criteria, or of a uniform hierarchy of criteria, that has played the major organizing role in the most authoritative and entrenched practices of reading—with the inevitable effect of repressing the difference and the specificity of other practices, casting them as naïve or exotic or perverse. Within a 'modernist' regime of value, commensuration between regimes (the application to diverse texts and reading practices of a single standard) can occur only by way of an absolute disvaluation of those practices that fail to measure up. When Umberto Eco, for example, constructs the concept of an 'average reader' of the James Bond texts who functions as a figure of literalness, he does so by ignoring the systems of cultural reference that structure popular readings. He simply misses many of the intertextual references (like the parody by the Bond films of other popular films, including earlier films in the Bond series) around which forms of popular 'knowingness' are constructed.[2] Eco

construes sophisticated reading as being subject to a distinctive form of social and cultural organization because he is familiar with

---

[2] Noel King reminds me, however, that Eco's book on Bond was written in the 1960s within a particular theoretical paradigm. His 'oversights' are not so much a matter of failure of insight as of the critical institution that draws a particular line between what should and what need not be known.

the determinations which organize it. Lacking such familiarity with the determinations which mould and configure popular reading, such reading is conceived as being socially and culturally unorganized. . . . [P]opular reading is conceived as a mere lack, characterized by the absence of the determinations which mould sophisticated reading.[3]

Alternatively, certain theorists who are in principle willing to grant the sheer difference between frameworks of value, their irreducibility to a single perspective, nevertheless seek to reserve some ultimate criterion which, 'in the last instance', allows for an absolute discrimination between more and less valuable texts. A favourite amongst semioticians is the criterion of informational complexity, understood as a purely formal and abstract criterion, by virtue of which some texts are more likely than others to be put to a multiplicity of uses and engage a multiplicity of quite divergent interests. But Barbara Herrnstein Smith is right, I think, to argue that among the competencies given by the acquisition of cultural capital is the ability to move between diverse cultural codes and to cope with, and indeed enjoy, structural complexity; thus the texts most highly valued by semioticians (and other intellectuals) 'will tend to be those that gratify the exercise of such competencies and engage interests of that kind'.[4] However desirable they might seem, such criteria are therefore by no means universal, and cannot form the basis of an aesthetic that could reconcile diverse criteria of value at a high level of abstraction.

As soon as it is conceded that there no longer exists a general economy of value, however, a series of difficult consequences comes into play.

For the category of value does not disappear with the collapse of a general economy;[5] it continues to organize every

[3] Tony Bennett and Janet Woollacott, *Bond and Beyond: The Political Career of a Popular Hero* (London and New York: Methuen, 1987), 79.
[4] *Contingencies of Value*, 51.
[5] The concept of value of course has a long genealogy in the disciplines of aesthetics and economics. Just as the category of labour, according to Marx, could achieve philosophical abstraction and generality only on the historical basis

local domain of the aesthetic and every aspect of daily life, from the ritualized discussions of movies or books or TV programmes through which relations of sociability are maintained, to the fine discriminations of taste in clothing or food or idiom that are made by every social class and every status subculture, to the organization of school and university curricula, museum and gallery exhibitions, and the allocation of commercial and public financing to the culture industries. There is no escape from the discourse of value, and no escape from the pressure and indeed the obligation to treat the world as though it were fully relational, fully interconnected. But what becomes entirely problematical is just the possibility of relation: that is, of critical movement across the spaces between *incommensurate* evaluative regimes. If the use of cultural objects is something more than a matter of individual preference (and the whole vocabulary of 'preference' as it is

of 'a very developed totality of real kinds of labour', so the category of value became a recognizable philosophical *problem* only under particular historical circumstances. John Guillory and Mary Poovey have each documented the emergence of the category of value in its modern aesthetic sense in the break-up of the discipline of moral philosophy (the key figure here is Adam Smith, and the disintegration of moral philosophy can be traced in the distance between the *Theory of Moral Sentiments* and *The Wealth of Nations*). What emerges, more precisely, is what Barbara Herrnstein Smith calls a 'double discourse of value': a relation of mutual exclusion between the autonomy of the aesthetic and the instrumentality of the commodity. This split is undermined almost from the beginning, however, by the reluctant or repressed recognition not only of the commodity status of artworks but also of the aesthetic dimension of commodities (Poovey takes *fashion* as the paradigm case of the constructedness of desire; its logic exposes 'both the persistence of aesthetic concerns within economic exchanges, and the persistence of a market logic in the domain of beauty or art'). Thus, Guillory argues, 'the "double discourse of value" is historically determined by the fact that while it is not possible for any object *not* to have a relation to the market, to the objective condition of universal commensuration, this relation cannot be defined by the simple reduction of the object (not even the commodity) to the quantum of exchange value'. This might suggest that that whole powerful tradition—including the work of Bataille and of Baudrillard—that opposes an economy of exchange to an economy of the gift, and the calculations of exchange value to the spontaneity of use value, is ultimately unworkable, because of the interpenetration of these two economies. Marx, *Grundrisse*, 104; John Guillory, *Cultural Capital: The Problem of Literary Canon Formation* (Chicago: University of Chicago Press, 1993), 325; Mary Poovey, 'Aesthetics and Political Economy in the Eighteenth Century', in George Levine and Carolyn Williams (eds.), *Aesthetics and Ideology* (New Brunswick, NJ: Rutgers University Press, forthcoming); Smith, *Contingencies of Value*, 127.

elaborated by the rationalist individualism of neoclassical economics simply begs the question of why different choices are made and of whether some choices are better than others; 'preference' has the great theoretical advantage of being ineffable),[6] then it becomes a problem to account for the systemic formation of value without assuming criteria that hold good right across the cultural field.

One possible strategy for dealing with this transformed economy would be through a move that seems, in fact, to get neatly beyond the whole problem of valuation. The move involves deciding that, rather than engaging *in* a discourse of value, calculating the relative worth of this text against that text according to some impossibly universal criterion of value, the job of the critic is rather to analyse the social relations of value themselves: to analyse the discourses of value, the socially situated frameworks of valuation from which value judgements are generated by readers. More broadly, this would be an analysis not only of norms and procedures but of the institutional structures through which value is formed, transmitted, and regulated; of the social distribution of literacy; of the mechanisms for the training and certification of valuing subjects; of the multiplicity of formations of value, differentiated by age, by class, by gender, by race, and so on.

Such a practice of dispassionate analysis, where normativity is passed from the subject to the object of study, has the virtue of generosity towards the very different, often contradictory discourses of value held by different groups; rather than privileging the values of an intellectual élite, proclaiming as universal a set of norms that can be demonstrated to be historically and culturally variable—norms of 'good taste' that are invariably class- and gender-specific—it concedes in advance the validity of the discrepant norms of other social groups: a validity that is now always relative to those groups and grounded in them, as are the norms of a socially situated high culture.

[6] Cf. John Fekete, 'Introductory Notes for a Postmodern Value Agenda', in John Fekete (ed.), *Life After Postmodernism: Essays on Value and Culture* (New York: St Martin's Press, 1987), p. viii.

Certainly this seems to me an indispensable first step in dealing with questions of value. It has the major flaw, however, of being unable to comprehend its own position, in ways that matter, within the ambit of its analysis. It is as though the understanding of value took place within some space that was free of social conflict, free of the play of interests, free of prejudice and misunderstanding; and as though (in a counter-movement to that passage of normativity from subject to object) the principle of totalization had been displaced from the object, the cultural field, to the self-effacing space of analysis itself. Methodological objectivism works as a denial of the principle that ' "culture" is always relational, an inscription of communicative processes that exist, historically, *between* subjects in relations of power'.[7]

Cultural studies has occasionally made the analogy between some of its own claims to disinterest and the procedures of ethnomethodology, in particular ethnomethodology's refusal of any position that would be external to the values and codes of the group, the *ethnos*, it is studying: its refusal, that is, of any metadiscourse. Indeed, because of ethnomethodology's bias in favour of practical, everyday sociological reasoning, professional sociology is given no privileged status whatsoever, and its procedures and its theoretical problems are of interest only as one more example of the use of reflexivity to construct and maintain a reality.

Given this absence of a privileged meta-level (since neither the sociologist nor the philosopher has any special claim to expertise denied to ordinary people, who are just as expert in the rules that govern social reality), there can be no *critique* of everyday processes: as Harold Garfinkel puts it, 'there can be nothing to quarrel with or to correct about practical sociological reasoning', and 'ethnomethodological studies are not

---

[7] James Clifford, 'Introduction: Partial Truths', in James Clifford and George E. Marcus (eds.), *Writing Culture: The Poetics and Politics of Ethnography* (Berkeley: University of California Press, 1986), 15.

directed to formulating or arguing correctives. They are useless when they are done as ironies.'[8]

Such a position seems to me to have clearly conservative political implications—at best it can give rise to a kind of political quietism. Nor does it seem to me even possible to avoid the practice of 'irony': to avoid, that is, the disaffected criticality of intellectual knowledge, since, as Bob Hodge and Alec McHoul argue in their analysis of the strategy of 'ethnomethodological indifference', although 'the text is supposed to speak for itself, untouched by sociological hands, it is nevertheless the case that the commentary—coming after the moment of action and data-collection—*gives the character of truth to its text*'.[9] Indeed, the very desire to avoid normative or prescriptive forms of reasoning inevitably leads to a repression of the privileged status of sociological enquiry, as well as its links to social power.

A further strategy closely related to this strategy of dispassionate analysis of value systems is the espousal or at least the acceptance of a kind of happy relativism: a model (which we might call 'postmodern') of the world as being irreducibly plural and informed by no principle of totalization.

Zygmunt Bauman, for example, sets up an opposition between two distinct modes of intellectual practice. On the one hand he posits a framework characteristic of modernity, according to which the orderly totality of the world is patterned by the uneven distribution of probabilities, and order is exerted by their manipulation. The stochastic nature of this universe thus implies no final chaos and no separation of knowledge from practice; on the contrary, 'effectivity of control and correctness [of knowledge] are tightly related (the second explains the first, the first corroborates the second), whether in laboratory experiment or societal practice'. On the other hand, there is what he calls the postmodern worldview of 'an unlimited number of models of order, each one

[8] Harold Garfinkel, *Studies in Ethnomethodology* (New Jersey: Prentice Hall, 1967), p. viii.
[9] Bob Hodge and Alec McHoul, 'The Politics of Text and Commentary', *Textual Practice*, 6: 2 (1992), 193–4.

guaranteed by a relatively autonomous set of practices. Order does not precede practices and hence cannot serve as an outside measure of their validity. Each of the many models of order makes sense solely in terms of the practices which validate it', and is upheld by the beliefs of a 'community of meanings'. These local forms of knowledge are not subject to any higher-level principle of explanation: 'there are no criteria for evaluating local practices which are situated outside traditions, outside "localities". Systems of knowledge may only be evaluated from "inside" their respective traditions.' Thus, 'if, from the modern point of view, relativism of knowledge was a problem to be struggled against and eventually overcome in theory and in practice, from the postmodern point of view relativity of knowledge (that is, its "embeddedness" in its own communally supported tradition) is a lasting feature of the world'.[10]

This 'postmodern' model continues to have the merit of openness towards the discrepant and often disdained structures of value of different social groups; in asserting the validity and the local specificity of a plurality of practices and codes of valuation it refuses to maintain the privilege of any one culture over any other. But this openness can easily become a kind of contempt in its own right, since it entails a certain indifference towards the otherness of other domains; no domain of value has anything to say to or about any other, and indeed there is an active prohibition on intercommunication; each domain is hermetically sealed from each of the others.

A more complex and more restless formulation of the problem of commensuration between heterogeneous value systems can be found in the work of Jean-François Lyotard. Following his turn, after the major texts of the early 1970s, from an energetics to a 'generalized rhetoric',[11] it is possible to isolate two main phases in this formulation.

---

[10] Bauman, *Legislators and Interpreters*, 3–4.
[11] Geoff Bennington, *Lyotard: Writing the Event* (Manchester: Manchester University Press, 1988), 117: 'Once the libidinal language is recognized as essentially that (a language), and can in principle become one more *dispositif*

The first is built around the concept of language games and the problematic of incommensurability between games that Lyotard derives from it. The form that Lyotard gives to this idea of an absence of measure is the postulate that the diversity of languages (including the diversity of ends informing them) cannot be reconciled at a higher logical level. Three different reasons are given to support this thesis. The least interesting, and the most dogmatically offered, is the argument that prescriptives cannot be derived from descriptives. The second has to do with the impossibility of transcending what he calls 'story' or 'opinion'[12] in order to attain a mode of understanding that could not itself be objectified as story.[13] The third reason is ethico-political rather than logical: it is an argument that the postulate of an integrating metadiscourse represents an attempt to impose discursive homogeneity where there not only is but ought to be heterogeneity. Far from constituting a problem, the diversity of language games is a prerequisite for the openness of the social system; conversely, the achievement of a 'consensus'—and therefore of an end to discussion—would represent a form of violence (or 'terror') done to the dynamic of social argument.

The mode of relativism that Lyotard describes in this phase of his work could perhaps be called an absolute relativism, and it generates precisely the contradictions implied by the oxymoron. As Samuel Weber observes of the argument of *Just*

rather than a general ground of explanation for all *dispositifs*, then a general field of "façons de parler" is opened up, which might be described in terms of a generalized rhetoric.'

[12] Cf. Jean-François Lyotard and Jean-Loup Thébaud, *Just Gaming*, trans. Wlad Godzich, Theory and History of Literature, Vol. 20 (Minneapolis: University of Minnesota Press, 1985), 43: 'We are always within opinion, and there is no possible discourse of truth on the situation. And there is no such discourse because one is caught up in a story, and one cannot get out of this story to take up a metalinguistic position from which the whole could be dominated. We are always immanent to stories in the making, even when we are the ones telling the story to the other.'

[13] Jean-François Lyotard, *The Differend: Phrases in Dispute*, trans. Georges Van Den Abbeele, Theory and History of Literature, Vol. 46 (Minneapolis: University of Minnesota Press, 1988), 138.

Gaming, where a universally binding prescriptive is formulated in order to maintain and underpin the value of singularity, 'the concept of absolute, intact singularity' remains 'tributary to the same logic of identity that sustains any and all ideas of totality'; and 'the concern with "preserving the purity" and singularity "of each game" by reinforcing its isolation from the others gives rise to exactly what was intended to be avoided: "the domination of one game by another", namely, the domination of the prescriptive'.[14]

The second 'phase' of Lyotard's later work (one that in part overlaps chronologically with the 'first') can be read as an attempt to overcome the insoluble problems that attach to any notion of *pure* heterogeneity, of *absolute* difference. Here, with the introduction of the concepts of the *différend* and of the genre of discourse, the question of the linkage (or 'slippage') between sentences displaces that of incommensurability—although the latter still remains the starting point for Lyotard's thinking. Whilst at one level translation between sentences belonging to different regimes continues not to be possible,[15] what is, however, not only possible but absolutely unavoidable is the linkage (*enchaînement*) of one sentence to another. The function of the genre of discourse is to bring sentences that may belong to quite distinct regimes within the ambit of a single end, a single teleology. It does not follow from this, however, that the incommensurability between sentences is eliminated or reconciled, since 'another genre of discourse can inscribe it into another finality. Genres of discourse do nothing more than shift the differend from the level of regimens to that of ends.'[16] And this process of reinscription, of shifting 'ends', is in principle endless.

---

[14] Samuel Weber, 'Afterword: Literature—Just Making It', in *Just Gaming*, 103, 104.

[15] In *Just Gaming* (pp. 53–4) Lyotard makes the distinction that 'languages are translatable, otherwise they are not languages; but language games are not translatable, because if they were, they would not be language games. It is as if one wanted to translate the rules and strategies of chess into checkers.' This makes it clear, of course, that non-translatability is part of the *definition* of language games.

[16] *The Differend*, 29.

One way of describing the movement in Lyotard's thought that is sketched here would be to say that there is a passage from an ontology of the sentence to a pragmatics of the sentence—to a concern with the uses to which sentences are put. Rather than formulating a general rule about the necessary separation of language games, Lyotard describes a process which encompasses both the practical commensuration of sentences as they are tied together by a discursive telos, and the endless dissociation of sentences as they are put to conflicting uses (or as there is conflict over the uses to which they may be put). This is to say that commensuration is possible (and is a practical necessity) not at the level of a metadiscourse that would somehow reconcile the semantic and pragmatic tensions between sentences, but at the more limited, 'local', and always contested level of the genre. It is not that there is no metadiscourse, but that there are many of them. If this conclusion ends by restating the problem of the lack of measure between distinct orders of knowledge and value (and if, as Connor notes, it continues to beg the question of the ground against which radical difference can be perceived),[17] it does so, nevertheless, no longer on the basis of an assertion of the self-contained purity of these orders, but in the recognition of the constant passage and the complex and conflictual transactions between them.

For Lyotard as for Wittgenstein, the entrenched separateness of language games is grounded in the specificity of the forms of life in which they are embedded.[18] What is at stake politically—at least for Lyotard—in this correlation is the irreducible diversity of human interests, and in particular a deep suspicion of any claim to represent a universally valid structure of interest—a claim typically made by the *particular*

[17] Steven Connor, *Theory and Cultural Value* (Oxford: Basil Blackwell, 1992), 112.

[18] There is a useful genealogy of the term *Lebensformen* as Wittgenstein found it 'in the air' in Vienna (most immediately among the neo-Kantian characterologists) in Allan Janik and Stephen Toulmin, *Wittgenstein's Vienna* (New York: Simon and Schuster, 1973), 230 ff.

class of intellectuals.[19] But much hangs on the way these two orders of being are bound together (and, indeed, on the conceptual separation made between them in the first place).

The problem is that of the forms of unity and identity ascribed to social groups; it is a problem that has been particularly acute for cultural studies, with its habitual reliance on a sociological relativism. At the limit, if aesthetic texts and practices of knowledge are closely tied to shared forms of life, and if their force is purely relative to these forms, then they are deprived of all except the most limited cognitive power—since they have no hold over any other domain. There is no scope for challenging the givenness of a cultural order: if every social group, every valuing community or subculture produces only those texts that express and validate its way of life, there is no *strong* ground from which to argue for alternative forms of textuality or indeed alternative ways of life.

A more general objection to the relativization of texts and codes of reading to communities, however, might be the organicism inherent in the notion of community itself: a concept that evokes the pre-industrial village rather than the abstract and highly mediated cultural spaces of the late twentieth century. The model of a plurality of valuing communities or subcultures is a model of a dispersed set of social clusters which are at once separate and self-contained; as John Guillory argues, the concept posits social identity as the basis for the solidarity of evaluation (and disagreement is therefore always a priori evidence of belonging to a different community: the argument is in this sense circular). Thus the

[19] In a discussion of racism, Immanuel Wallerstein has made an explicit claim that the value of universality is specific to the small class of 'cadres', whereas 'by assuming a particularist stance—whether of class, of nation or of race—the working strata are expressing an instinct of self-protection against the ravages of a universalism that must be hypocritical within a system founded both on the permanence of inequality and on the process of material and social polarization'. Étienne Balibar and Immanuel Wallerstein, *Race, Nation, Class: Ambiguous Identities* (London: Verso, 1991), 230. I think it is possible to accept that this argument is correct without thereby being driven to abandon all aspiration to the achievement of 'universal' values.

concept of value cannot adequately account for differences of judgement *within* a valuing community, since it is used above all to 'exalt the difference of the community from other communities'.[20]

It is probably not, I think, any longer problematic to say that value is always *value-for*, always tied to some valuing group; what does raise a problem is the fact that in our world the boundaries of communities are always porous, since most people belong to many valuing communities simultaneously; since communities overlap; and since they're heterogeneous. Moreover, to tie texts to forms of life in this way assumes that texts enter exhaustively into their context, without residue, and without the possibility of further, unpredicted, and perhaps unpredictable uses being made of them. The concept of community in cultural studies works as an *archè*, an organic and unifying origin.

Janice Radway speaks of the naturalization of presence inherent in the comparable concept of an empirical 'audience', and hence of the difficulty of theorizing 'the dispersed, anonymous, unpredictable nature of the use of mass-produced, mass-mediated cultural forms', where the receivers of such forms 'are never assembled fixedly on a site or even in an easily identifiable space' and 'are frequently not uniformly or even attentively disposed to systems of cultural production, or to the messages they issue'.[21]

But rather than adopting her tactic of attempting an even more exhaustive empirical analysis, a total ethnography, of 'the ever-shifting kaleidoscope of cultural circulation and consumption',[22] it seems to me more useful (and more economical) to posit a mediating institutional mechanism to account both for the diversity of value and for the absence of any simple or necessary coincidence between social groups and the structure of valuation.

---

[20] Guillory, *Cultural Capital*, 278.
[21] Janice Radway, 'Reception Study: Ethnography and the Problems of Dispersed Audiences and Nomadic Subjects', *Cultural Studies*, 2: 3 (1988), 361.
[22] Ibid.

The concept I want to propose is that of the *regime of value*, a semiotic institution generating evaluative regularities under certain conditions of use, and in which particular empirical audiences or communities may be more or less fully imbricated. Arjun Appadurai uses the concept in this sense to define the cultural framework within which very variable investments are made in the exchange of commodities. Adopting from Simmel the notion that economic value has no general existence but is always the particular result of 'the commensuration of two intensities of demand', and that this commensuration takes the form of 'the exchange of sacrifice and gain', he argues that it is thus exchange that underlies the formation of value, and exchange occurs within specific regimes where 'desire and demand, reciprocal sacrifice and power interact to create economic value in specific social situations'.[23] Regimes of value are mechanisms that permit the construction and regulation of value-equivalence, and indeed permit cross-cultural mediation. Thus the concept

does *not* imply that every act of commodity exchange presupposes a complete cultural sharing of assumptions, but rather that the degree of value coherence may be highly variable from situation to situation, and from commodity to commodity. A regime of value, in this sense, is consistent with both very high and very low sharing of standards by the parties to a particular commodity exchange. Such regimes of value account for the constant transcendence of cultural boundaries by the flow of commodities, where culture is understood as a bounded and localized system of meanings.   (p. 15)

The regime of value constitutes 'a broad set of agreements concerning what is desirable, what a reasonable "exchange of sacrifices" comprises, and who is permitted to exercise what kind of effective demand in what circumstances' (p. 57); this regulation is always political in its mediation of discrepant interests.

[23] Arjun Appadurai, 'Introduction: Commodities and the Politics of Value', in Arjun Appadurai (ed.), *The Social Life of Things: Commodities in Cultural Perspective* (Cambridge: Cambridge University Press, 1986), 4.

The concept is roughly similar to Tony Bennett's concept of the *reading formation*, which is likewise used to bypass a sociological realism that would tie modes of reading directly to social groups. The reading formation is a semiotic apparatus, a 'set of discursive and intertextual determinations that organize and animate the practice of reading, connecting texts and readers in specific relations to one another by constituting readers as reading subjects of particular types and texts as objects-to-be-read in particular ways'.[24] What this means is that neither texts nor readers have an existence independent of these relations; that every act of reading, and hence every act of ascribing value, is specific to the particular regime that organizes it. Texts and readers are not separable elements with fixed properties but 'variable functions within a discursively ordered set of relations',[25] and apparently identical texts and readers will function quite differently within different regimes.

Regimes of value are thus relatively autonomous of and have no directly expressive relation to social groups. In the case of 'high'-cultural regimes, this relative autonomy is an effect of historical survivals and of the relative autonomy of the modern educational apparatus, both of which then give rise to interpretative and evaluative traditions that do not directly reflect class interests; in the case of 'popular' regimes, their relative autonomy has less to do with the historical persistence of codes of value (although this is still a factor) than with the way the mass media work to form audiences that cross the borders of classes, ethnic groups, genders, and indeed nations. The concept of regime expresses one of the fundamental theses of work in cultural studies: that no object, no text, no cultural practice has an intrinsic or necessary meaning or value or function; and that meaning, value, and function are always the effect of specific (and changing, changeable) social relations and mechanisms of signification.

[24] Tony Bennett, 'Texts in History: The Determinations of Readings and Their Texts', *Journal of the Midwest Modern Language Association*, 18: 1 (1985), 7.
[25] Ibid. 10.

Thus the regimes that make up the domain of 'high' culture consist of sets of interlocking institutions framing particular kinds of practice and producing certain axiological regularities: school curricula; classroom trainings in appropriate responses and evaluations; the certification of academic expertise and the structure of professional careers in cultural production and cultural criticism; the institutions of the theatre, the concert hall, the museum, and the art gallery; the art market; the publishing industry (and the 'quality' niches within it); specialist and non-specialist journals and magazines; criticism and reviews in the *feuilleton* sections of newspapers and of radio and television programming; peer-group cultures, and the conversational rituals that sustain evaluative codes; particular patterns of work and leisure, and particular codes of status-discrimination; and so on. As the composition of this network, together with the protocols and criteria by which value is articulated, vary historically, so too do the particular functions performed by 'high' culture (*one* of these, but not the only one, may be to reinforce the discrepancy between aesthetic and economic discourses of value, as a way of designating aesthetic—that is, non-economic—value as a marker of status).

Like the regimes of high culture, although often in less self-assertive ways, the regimes of 'popular' culture too tend to take on the task of reinforcing the disjunction between the two discourses of value—the task of converting commodities into non-economic values (aesthetic values, which may however take an ethical and experiential form). And they too are organized around complex apparatuses of codification, of formal or informal trainings, and of status marking. There may well, of course, be regimes of value whose central principle is the inappropriateness of 'evaluation'; Eric Michaels makes this case for the Australian Aboriginal art of the Western desert, which is based on a principle of reproduction and on inherited authorship rights,[26] and similar arguments have been made for some forms of

---

[26] Eric Michaels, 'Bad Aboriginal Art', *Art and Text*, 28 (1988), 59–73.

postmodernist art. The point, though, is that even such an ethos of non-evaluation must be organized and regulated by a definite and historically particular regime.

An essay on graffiti by Susan Stewart neatly crystallizes the different framings and consequences that arise when a cultural form is positioned by different evaluative regimes.[27] As an 'indigenous or folk form carried out by a community of writers relatively homogeneous in age (9–16)' (p. 165) the practice of graffiti-writing in New York and Philadelphia situates itself in one sense firmly outside 'the aesthetic' and within a politics of the (re-)appropriation of space; in another sense, however, it is practised in accordance with quite specifically aesthetic codes. It possesses a comprehensive vocabulary of evaluation (an anti-language which often inverts the standard terms of approval, and which, giving special weight to the criteria of difficulty and frequency, values 'elegance, speed, grace, and the sensuality of the body') (p. 171); and a distinctive technical vocabulary to describe its tools and its activities. A well-defined hierarchy of practitioners structures a semi-formal apprenticeship system:

beginners (called 'toys') work with master writers as apprentices. The toy generally progresses from writing simple 'tags' (signatures made with markers or spray paints) on any surface to writing 'throw-ups' (larger tags thrown onto inaccessible surfaces or the outsides of subway cars) to writing 'pieces' (short for masterpieces: symbolic and/or figurative works such as landscapes, objects, letters, or characters drawn on a variety of surfaces). (p. 165)

The dominant code is one of stylistic individuation, expressed in the triumphant formalization of handwriting and repeated insistently across public space in such a way as to 'serve purely as a mark of presence, the concrete evidence of an individual existence and the reclamation of the environment through the label of the personal' (p. 165). The investment in frequency of production is borrowed from

---

[27] Susan Stewart, 'Ceci Tuera Cela: Graffiti as Crime and Art', in John Fekete (ed.), *Life After Postmodernism: Essays on Value and Culture* (New York: St Martin's Press, 1987), 161–80; references will be given in the text.

advertising and publicity, and the act of writing is 'a tautological process of self-promotion miming the reflexive signifiers of advertising and "packaging"'; the borrowing should however be read, Stewart argues, as 'a matter of adaptation, manipulation, and localization' (p. 166). For this aesthetics of the signature works both within and against commodity culture, figuring the writer at once as brand name and as the repetition of resistance to the repetitions of commodity culture.

Whereas, for the writers, graffiti works[28] as an appropriation of privatized public space, a reduction of the public-monumental to the scale of the handwritten name, which 'contrast[s] to the monument's abstraction and stasis the signature's personality, mobility, and vernacular, localized audience' (p. 169), within a quite different regime of value—that which organizes the readings of city officials—graffiti relates to public space as dirt and crime. A key term here is 'defacement': as with the defacement of coinage, graffiti 'is considered a threat to the entire system of meanings by which [public] surfaces acquire value, integrity, and significance' (p. 168). Specifically, it is a threat to the system of property values, and a mark of the failure of state policing of the common domain.

It thus ties into a wider semiotic network in which it is read as an ethico-political, not as an aesthetic, practice. Explicitly placed outside the realm of the cultural, it is linked to 'the dirty, the animal, the uncivilized, and the profane' (p. 168). Its producers are (incorrectly) assumed all to be of Afro-American or Latin descent, and are characterized as deviant (members of criminal gangs, or even insane). Despite the absence of a sexual thematics in graffiti, which focuses entirely on the representation of the proper name, it is organized within this regime as an *obscene* form: writing in the wrong place. And, in order that the vast resources expended on 'graffiti maintenance' can be legitimated, it is characterized,

---

[28] I have followed Stewart, and common usage, in treating 'graffiti' as a singular collective noun.

despite its physical durability, as a reversible or erasable form: like dirt, and unlike the artwork, it contains within it the necessity of its own removal.

The conflict between these two axiological regimes is fought out at the level of the streets and the subways. A third regime, however, moves the scene of value off the streets and into the coffee-table books and the galleries. Stewart describes two wings, the 'liberal' and the 'avant-garde', of the aesthetic appropriation of graffiti (the difference between them is a matter of a family quarrel within the knowledge class). The liberal solution to the 'graffiti problem' involves one of two demands: either that writers paint over their work, or that they become art students, redeploying their talents in the traditional studio genres. Stewart calls these approaches 'insidious': the ' "encouragement" of the writer's creativity is in effect a matter of disciplinary punishment, a punishment that takes as its thematic a generalized representation and simultaneous suppression of the signature which had been at the centre of the graffiti artist's work' (p. 170). To 'reform' the writers of graffiti—to channel their skills into the codes of a discrepant aesthetic formation through a process of retraining—is at once an aesthetic and a political project, one that involves a repression of the social conditions of necessity and possibility of graffiti writing and a determined attempt to keep up appearances.

The avant-garde aesthetic, by contrast, seeks to retain the signature of the writer, but to retain it in the fetishized and saleable mode of 'a self-conscious intentionality which places the artist intertextually within the tradition as it is defined by critics and the art establishment in general' (p. 172). This tradition (that of 'a progression of individual artefacts worked by individual masters') (ibid.) displaces the local and recent culture of autograph graffiti into a place where it figures as 'the spontaneous, the primitive, the real of this tradition—a real located in nature and the body. Here the invention of a tradition for graffiti, particularly as a form of "folk art", is the invention of both nostalgia and currency. Graffiti is valued as a dying art form, the romantic heir to abstract expressionism and pop art' (p. 173). The movement to a regime of *taste* substitutes a new object—graffiti produced on canvas as an object of appreciation—for the mobile and difficult autograph on the subway car, or the logo rapidly inscribed on the side of a bank. Within this regime, 'the valuation of graffiti is an effort to accommodate through adaptation a novel threat to the status of the art object in general. To the extent that graffiti writers move off the street and into the gallery, the threat will be met' (p. 174).

A final regime of value—one that brackets the status of graffiti as art in order to refuse a 'liberal pluralism of aesthetic judgements' (p. 163) according to which each regime confronts the 'same' object from different perspectives—is that somewhat less visible regime from within which Stewart herself writes, and which makes it possible for her to play off the 'street' regime against the others. Like the aesthetic regime, its conditions of existence are the possession of extensive cultural capital; it differs, perhaps, in its greater ability to elaborate a distance from immediate class interests (or, to put this differently, in its prosecution of an alternative set of interests).

The concept of regimes of value makes two things possible. First, by specifying the *mechanism* by means of which 'extratextual' determinations like social position are translated into reading practices (mechanisms of training in the recognition and use of distinct codes of value) and the formal or informal institutions within which they operate, it demonstrates the irreducibility of semiotic codes to class or race or age or gender—and, conversely, it stresses the point that, because of this very non-equivalence, class and race and age and gender are always to an important degree imagined (but not imaginary) structures. Second, it makes it possible to rethink the relation between canonical (or 'high') and non-canonical (or 'popular') culture, as *practices* of value rather than as collections of texts with a necessary coherence: the text of graffiti can figure just as well within a 'high'-cultural regime as within a 'popular' regime. This is not to revert to a use of these categories as *substantive* or internally coherent categories; it is merely to accept the fact that the concepts of a 'high' and a 'popular' regime continue to organize the cultural field and to produce ideological effects of cultural distinction. (At the same time, this shift from texts to practices underlines the spuriousness of those defences of 'the canon' which assume that texts have intrinsic worth.)

Judgements of value are always choices made within a particular regime. This is not to say that the regime determines which judgement will be made, but that it specifies a particular range of possible judgements, and a particular set of appropriate criteria; in setting an agenda, it also excludes certain criteria and certain judgements as inappropriate or unthinkable. Regimes therefore allow for disagreement, specifying the terms within which it can be enacted. Disagreement may also take place in the space of overlap between regimes, or between discrepant and non-intersecting regimes; but in a sense disagreement is only ever really possible where *some* agreement on the rules of engagement can be held in common.

If commensurability of criteria within a regime enables both concurrent and divergent judgements to be made, the incommensurability of criteria *between* regimes thus tends to preclude the possibility of productive exchange. Disagreement of this kind can be settled by an agreement to disagree, or by the attempt to impose one set of criteria over another. The latter has traditionally been the way of high culture and its institutions, if only because those institutions have had the power to do so; and the universalization of high-cultural values may take the shape either of a discrediting of other criteria of value, or of an appropriation of those criteria.

The difficulties that arise from any attempt to avoid the politics of totalizing judgement are often cast in terms of the philosophical dilemma of axiological (and, by implication, epistemological) relativism. At their core lies, I think, the anxiety generated by the fiction that is strategically posited by any politically informed relativism: the fiction that, in order to neutralize my own inevitable partiality, I should consider all domains of value to be *formally* equivalent. (This, it should be noted, is also the fiction put into place by any democratic electoral system: that, however passionately I may believe in the rightness of one party, I must suspend this belief in order to recognize the formal right of any other political party to win power, and, conversely, to accept as politically legitimate the possibility that my party will lose. This suspension of belief, for all its apparent ordinariness in the established democracies, depends upon a sophisticated politics of know-ledge.)[29] What causes anxiety is a belief that recognition of the equal right of other values to *formal* (but not necessarily substantive) respect implies that all values or arguments must therefore be considered equally 'valid'; and that this means that all arguments, by being held equal, are thus in some sense trivialized. Arguments, on this reading, cannot be defended or adjudicated because there is no possibility of winning an argument.

One response to this would be to elaborate a theory of what it means for an argument or a value to be *locally* valid: that is, for it to be judged correct or incorrect within a specific and limited framework, where such a judgement is entirely appropriate, but beyond which it ceases to hold any force. But Barbara Herrnstein Smith is on stronger ground in refusing the terms of the dilemma altogether. If the concepts of validity and objectivity, which continue to be presupposed by the arguments against relativism, are rejected as vacuous, this by no means entails that judgements of value cannot be evaluated and said to be better or worse (just as Foucault's argument that judgements of truth and falsity are always generated within a particular regime of truth does not mean that he himself will not make such judgements within a particular regime). What is entailed is that judgements of value and truth are relative to a social position of enunciation

[29] Cf. Adam Przeworski, *Democracy and the Market: Political and Economic Reforms in Eastern Europe and Latin America* (Cambridge: Cambridge University Press, 1991), 93. In making this analogy I do not want to downplay the extent to which political choice in most of the established democracies has become virtually meaningless.

and to a set of conditions of enunciation (which are not necessarily the same for each instance of an utterance). 'Better' and 'worse' will be meaningful terms to the extent that a framework of valuation is agreed, and that the authority of speakers is accepted, at least provisionally, within it.

Nevertheless, neither of these responses confronts the question of how it is possible to make judgements across the boundaries of regimes. The analogy between the strategic fictions deployed by axiological relativism and by political democracy can perhaps serve to clarify the limits of the former, since these fictions belong to a larger historical framework. Both the rational valuing subject and the citizen endowed with rights and with formal equality before the law are aspects of the bourgeois subject of legal contract, a figure that integrates the dimensions of rational economic calcula-tion, ethical integrity, consistency of will over time, and positional equality within and for the duration of the contractual framework.[30] The figure of the bourgeois subject (I use the concept in a historically specific sense) is neither a pure illusion nor a straightforward social gain, since the formal equalities on which it is predicated are always systematically interwoven with, and work to conceal, structural inequalities in the economic sphere and the actual control of the legal and political spheres by the dominant class. Relativism of value and of knowledge is closely connected with—and is perhaps even a logical extrapolation from—this structure of formal equality; and this connection, which is *formally* 'progressive', indicates both its political usefulness (it is not a position from which we can ever afford to retreat, out of nostalgia for a social order, past or future, free of these fictions), and its limitations. In so far as cognitive relativism posits a plurality of equivalent spheres, it necessarily fails to conceive of inequalities and asymmetries between these spheres (and therefore leaves the existing distribution of power untouched); and it is likely to

---

[30] Cf. Betty Mensch, 'Freedom of Contract as Ideology', *Stanford Law Review*, 33 (Apr. 1981), 753–92; Roberto Mangabeira Unger, *The Critical Legal Studies Movement* (Cambridge, Mass.: Harvard University Press, 1986), 63 ff.

conceptualize valuing communities in terms of self-contained positional identities, such that difference is posited between rather than within spheres of value.

In order to move beyond the limitations of relativism (which does not mean the reinstatement of some non-positional perspective), it becomes necessary to redefine the notion of positionality itself, together with the notion of representation on which it depends. The crucial argument here, it seems to me, is the one that follows when regimes of value are detached from a directly expressive relation to a social community. To speak is then never quite the same thing as 'to express the interests of' or 'to stand for' a particular group. At the same time, the dissociation of regime from group means that it is likely that members of any group will belong to more than one regime of value. This is particularly the case with 'cultural' intellectuals, who are specifically trained in the ability to switch codes, to move readily between different practices of reading and of valuation.

Two sets of questions branch out from these difficult and intricate problems of positionality. The first is a set of practical difficulties within the cultural institutions. Given the fact (if this is conceded) of incommensurability between different regimes of value, and given the intense social interests that play around these fractures and asymmetries, how is it possible for judgements of value to be applied in the routine and everyday manner required by school and university curricula, by editorial decision-making, by decisions about arts funding and research funding, and about the exhibition of artefacts? What gets floor-space and wall-space in the museum and the gallery? What gets discussed in the arts pages of the newspapers and magazines? What do we teach our students: the canonical texts (whose authority they cannot otherwise fight against because they do not know them)? non-canonical texts (and don't these then become precisely an alternative *canon*)?[31] some mix of the two—and if so, then

---

[31] 'What should have been clear before now is that the canonizing effect does not in the least require a stable corpus of works in which to be embodied. Since

according to which criteria do we choose?[32] Is it possible to bypass the uncanny symbiosis of 'high' culture and 'popular' culture, their mutually reinforcing sacralization, in order to make possible a continual estrangement of the frames within which texts are normally and normatively read? Is it *practically* possible, as Steven Connor proposes, to live with 'the paradoxical structure of value as immanent transcendence',[33] a system of contingent universals—and indeed, is it 'practically' possible not to?[34] These are questions not just about criteria, but about whose stories get told, and, crucially, about who gets to make these decisions, who doesn't, and on what grounds.

In the first instance, of course, these are questions not about individual decisions but about institutional structures. Training in the protocols of reading and in the formulation of value is received in part in the institutions of mass education and mass culture, which are detached from local cultures and local communities; and which are, in that sense, and in that sense only, 'universal'. These are the institutions controlled by the knowledge class—the class of intellectuals in the broadest sense of the term.[35]

canonization depends not on what one says about texts, so much as where one says it from, there is no real reason why a postmodernist world of shifting or open canons need do anything to the canonizing effect of discourses within institutions, except perhaps to make them ideologically more subtle and inconspicuous.' Steven Connor, 'The Modern and the Postmodern as History', *Essays in Criticism*, XXXVII: 3 (1987), 188; cf. Guillory, *Cultural Capital*, 81: 'The movement to open or expand the canon might be regarded, among other things, as a belated attempt to save the bourgeois sociolect by expanding its base of textual representation.'

[32] For an extended analysis of the problems that arise from such basic pedagogic questions, cf. Charlotte Brunsdon, 'Problems with Quality', *Screen*, 31: 1 (1990), 67–90.

[33] Connor, *Theory and Cultural Value*, 33.

[34] Cf. ibid. 2: 'It is both the desire for an absolute grounding of political practice, and the attempt to imagine a political practice without grounding, which are hopelessly impractical and unresponsive to the practical complexity attaching to questions of value.'

[35] Bruce Robbins has useful things to say about the profession of literary studies, *qua* profession, in *Secular Vocations: Intellectuals, Professionalism, Culture* (London: Verso, 1993).

At this point, then, I return to the question of the 'interests' of intellectuals: that is, above all, their institutional interest in cultural capital and its distribution. I shall use what I take to be an unresolved problem in a passage of Andrew Ross's *No Respect*[36] as a way of getting at the articulation of this interest with the institutional distinction between high and low culture.

Ross begins the passage, towards the end of the book, with a concise argument about the effects of distinction brought about by the disdain felt by high-cultural intellectuals for popular culture: 'the exercise of cultural taste, wherever it is applied today, remains one of the most efficient guarantors of anti-democratic power relations, and, when augmented by the newly stratified privileges of a knowledge society, gives rise to new kinds of subordination' (p. 227). No longer just the lackeys of the ruling class, intellectuals are themselves the holders of significant social power which is manifested precisely in the exercise of judgement. To intellectual 'disdain' Ross counterposes popular 'disrespect':

Intellectuals today are unlikely to recognize . . . what is fully at stake in the new *politics of knowledge* if they fail to understand why so many cultural forms, devoted to horror and porn, and steeped in chauvinism and other bad attitudes, draw their popular appeal from expressions of disrespect for the lessons of educated taste. The sexism, racism, and militarism that pervades these genres is never expressed in a pure form (whatever that might be); it is articulated through and alongside social resentments born of subordination and exclusion. A politics that only preaches about the sexism, racism, and militarism while neglecting to rearticulate the popular, resistant appeal of the disrespect will not be a popular politics and will lose ground in any contest with the authoritarian populist languages that we have experienced under Reaganism and Thatcherism.

And Ross goes on to warn that

for many intellectuals, such a politics has always been and still is difficult to imagine, let alone accept, because of its necessary

[36] Andrew Ross, *No Respect: Intellectuals and Popular Culture* (London and New York: Routledge, 1989). Page references are given in the text.

engagement with aggressively indifferent attitudes toward the life of the mind and the protocols of knowledge; because it appeals to the body in ways which cannot always be trusted; and because it trades on pleasures which a training in political rationality encourages us to devalue. But the challenge of such a politics is greater than ever because in an age of expert rule, the popular is perhaps the one field in which intellectuals are least likely to be experts.   (pp. 231–2)

This argument is the culmination of a book that meticulously documents the ways in which the notion of 'the popular' has served as an emblem by means of which North American intellectuals, and indeed intellectuals elsewhere in the world, have figured their relation to an imaginary Other. To take one case, for 1950s left intellectuals like Sydney Finkelstein and Eric Hobsbawm, American jazz 'had become the ideal embodiment of an authentic music by the people, for the people'; and

similar claims for the authenticity of an organic communitarian culture would also be made in the subsequent course of rock music by musicians, youth leaders, and pop critics at the height of the equally short-lived rock counterculture in the late sixties. But the period of jazz's authentic 'moment' as a legitimate populist art, from the late forties of Finkelstein to the late fifties of Hobsbawm, no longer belonged to the large, popular audience it had once enjoyed. Instead, it belonged to traditional intellectuals in possession, finally, of their Holy Grail, and, increasingly, to the organic black intellectual voices of musicians.   (p. 93)

In developing this argument through a series of case studies—the cultural politics of the Popular Front, the Cold War critique of mass culture, Pop Art and camp, the feminist anti-pornography movement—Ross is scrupulous not to counterpose intellectual constructions of the popular to some more authentic mode of popular consumption. Contrasting the North American with the European appropriation of American popular culture, he says:

While the American experience of commercial popular culture was, of course, much more *lived* and direct, we should not fall into the trap of assuming that it was less mediated or fantasmatic. The uses

made of comic strips, science fiction, 'Detroit' styling, Westerns,
rock'n'roll, advertising, etc., by different social groups cannot be
read as if they were spontaneous responses to real social conditions.
On the contrary, they represent an imaginary relation to these
conditions, and one which is refracted through the powerful lens of
the so-called American Dream—a pathologically seductive infusion
of affluence, sublimated ordinariness and achieved utopian pleasure.
The American as a dream American.   (p. 149)

The very cogency of Ross's analysis, however, makes it
difficult to understand just how to take his urging that
intellectuals must learn to 'engage' with the anti-intellectualism of popular culture. On the one hand, this appeal assumes
(although Ross qualifies this assumption elsewhere) that the
power of the knowledge class is in some sense the dominant
social power, and it thereby both underplays the dominant
role of capital (intellectuals may run the schools and the mass
media, but they do not own them), and accepts what may be a
kind of scapegoating of intellectuals. At the same time, Ross
offers no indications of how, or from what political position,
such an 'engagement' might be possible without a repetition
of that imaginary identification in which intellectuals have
constructed 'the popular' as a fantasy of otherness. There are
clear limits to the extent to which it is possible for intellectuals
to associate themselves with anti-intellectualism; and there are
limits to how far they can or should suspend their critique of,
for example, racism, sexism, and militarism. By the same
token, Ross begs the question of the bad faith that might be
involved in intellectuals identifying with a position that
directly attacks their own status and activity, including that
very act of identification. There are, after all, already strong
traditions of intellectual anti-intellectualism in the United
States (and elsewhere), exemplified currently by those New
Right intellectuals who identify a 'politically correct' liberal
intelligentsia as the holders of real social power.

Let me put in the deliberately exaggerated form of a double-
bind the central aporia that I see for cultural studies in
confronting these questions of value: the impossibility either
of espousing, in any simple way, the norms of high culture, in

so far as this represents that exercise of distinction which works to exclude those not possessed of cultural capital; or, on the other hand, of espousing, in any simple way, the norms of 'popular' culture to the extent that this involves, for the possessors of cultural capital, a fantasy of otherness and a politically dubious will to speak on behalf of this imaginary Other.

Despite its exaggerated form, this dilemma is, I think, a real one, and one that we should not seek to resolve too quickly; it speaks to the heart of the political difficulty of being a cultural intellectual in a world where culture is defined by its relation to one or another market in distinction. It is a dilemma that may not necessarily take the form of personal anxiety—indeed, a postmodern floating between cultural regimes may be deeply pleasurable—but it poses difficult questions about pedagogic strategy, about political effectivity, and about the organization of cultural institutions.

My intention in posing the dilemma in this way is not to argue that intellectuals should keep their distance from popular culture, but to argue that they should not idealize it as their mystical Other, precisely because they themselves are not separate from this Other. As Larry Grossberg argues:

We are always and already one (if not many) of the masses. Consequently, we cannot start by dividing up the terrain according to our own maps of tastes and distastes (although our travelogues are always contaminated by them), or our own sense of some imaginary boundary which divides a mythic (and always dominant) mainstream from a magical (and always resisting or reflexive) marginality, or our own notion of an assumed gulf between our intellectual self and our popular-media self.[37]

The overlap between regimes of value is the condition that makes it possible to move between incommensurate regimes, at the same time as it both produces and frustrates the will to totalizing judgement. One possible model for such a process of crossover between regimes organized by incompatible

[37] Lawrence Grossberg, 'Wandering Audiences, Nomadic Critics', *Cultural Studies*, 2: 3 (1988), 385.

criteria perhaps already exists, in the rather routine form of the study of literary texts from different historical periods: in the form, that is, not just of an analysis of historically differentiated norms of production and reception, but of a refusal either completely to privilege the present (making its categories the standard of familiarity from which the strangeness of other historical categories deviates) or completely to forget it (so that history becomes unhistorical in its pure estrangement from present interests). This is the model of a hermeneutics, understood not as a method of depth interpretation but as the mediation of interpretative frameworks. I invoke this model not in order to suggest that a ready-made and properly functioning paradigm for cultural studies exists elsewhere,[38] nor to announce a new set of scholarly tasks, but simply to indicate one of the ways in which an openness to cultural difference might be compatible with an established and regularized methodology, rather than being a matter of unreproducible spontaneity.

One other key locus for the experience, or rather the construction, of otherness as a central disciplinary moment is of course ethnography. This is a model which has had an increasing influence on cultural studies, though often in ways that reflect little knowledge of ethnographic procedures[39] or the complexity of ethnography's own methodological reflection (in recent years, for example, its problematization of the forms of writing through which the object of ethnography is formed as at once exotic and familiar).[40] The exemplary

[38] I have made detailed criticisms of Gadamerian hermeneutics in *Marxism and Literary History* (Cambridge, Mass. and Oxford: Harvard University Press and Basil Blackwell, 1986), 224–7.

[39] Cf. Nightingale, 'What's "Ethnographic" about Ethnographic Audience Research?', 50–63.

[40] James Clifford and George E. Marcus (eds.), *Writing Culture: The Poetics and Politics of Ethnography* (Berkeley: University of California Press, 1986); James Clifford, *The Predicament of Culture: Twentieth-Century Ethnography, Literature, and Art* (Cambridge, Mass.: Harvard University Press, 1988); George E. Marcus and Michael M. J. Fischer (eds.), *Anthropology as Cultural Critique: An Experimental Moment in the Human Sciences* (Chicago: University of Chicago Press, 1986); Clifford Geertz, *Works and Lives: The Anthropologist as Author* (Stanford, Calif.: Stanford University Press, 1988); Edward Said, 'Representing the Colonized: Anthropology's Interlocutors', *Critical Inquiry*, 15

aspect of ethnography in this context, however, must surely be no more than the brute fact of its complicity with colonial (and neo-colonial, and post-colonial) domination.[41]

The second set of questions is separate from but directly connected to the first set. They are ethical and political questions: who speaks? who speaks for whom? whose voice is listened to, whose voice is spoken over, who has no voice? whose claim to be powerless works as a ruse of power? under what circumstances is it right or wrong, effective or ineffective, to speak for others? And how can relations of enunciative power—which by definition are shifting and situational—adequately be described?

A recent essay by Linda Alcoff may serve as a point of entry to these questions of representation (in both senses of the word).[42] Alcoff casts the question of representation in terms of enunciative modality, the relation between social position and the semantics of utterance. Beginning with the 'growing recognition that where one speaks from alters the truth of what one says, and thus that one cannot assume an ability to transcend one's location', she then extends this on the one hand to the argument that 'the practice of privileged persons speaking for or on behalf of less privileged persons has actually resulted (in many cases) in increasing or reinforcing the oppression of the group spoken for' (pp. 6–7), and on the other hand (shifting from persons to discursive positions) to the thesis that 'certain contexts and locations are allied with structures of oppression, and certain others are allied with resistance to oppression. Therefore all are not politically equal, and, given that politics is connected to truth, all are not epistemically equal' (p. 15).

(1989), 205–25; Johannes Fabian, *Time and the Other: How Anthropology Makes Its Object* (New York: Columbia University Press, 1983).

[41] Is it necessary to add that this is in no way meant to impugn the integrity of practising anthropologists, or to overlook the sensitivity that the discipline has developed to the relations of power that hold between it and the peoples it studies? The criticism is structural and historical, and it draws to a large extent upon a political critique developed within the profession itself.

[42] Linda Alcoff, 'The Problem of Speaking for Others', *Cultural Critique*, 20 (1991–2), 5–32; further references will be given in the text.

Alcoff's aim is to produce something like an ethics, or an ethico-politics, of speaking. Her argument is complicated, however, by the collapse, during the course of the essay, of the solidity of the concept of position (or 'context' or 'social location'). Thus she concedes that the notion of social location cannot be used as an index of determinant origin, since speakers can never be said to be fully in control of the meanings of utterances, and certainly have little control over the uses that are made of them. To be an 'author' is not to be the source of an utterance, but rather to be *credited* as its source; and the import of an utterance cannot be deduced simply from its propositional content or from the enunciative position or credentials of its speaker, since the utterance will also generate an open-ended chain of effects which is not reducible to either of those two moments.

In order to retrieve from this concession some of the force of the concept of enunciative modality—but also to guard against the converse danger of the *reduction* of meaning to social position—Alcoff introduces a more qualified model of the semantics of context: location 'bears on' meaning and truth rather than determining them, and it is multiple and mobile. The act of speaking from within a group is consequently 'immensely complex. To the extent that location is not a fixed essence, and to the extent that there is an uneasy, underdetermined, and contested relationship between location on the one hand and meaning and truth on the other, we cannot reduce evaluation of meaning and truth to a simple identification of the speaker's location' (pp. 16–17).

Moreover, even so far as the thesis linking a privileged right and competence to speak with symbolic oppression holds good, the appropriate response to this link is not necessarily to abdicate from speaking for others. For two reasons: first, because such a response 'assumes that one *can* retreat into one's own discrete location and make claims entirely and singularly based on that location that do not range over others'; and second, because 'even a complete retreat from speech is of course not neutral since it allows the continued dominance of current discourses and acts by omission to reinforce their dominance' (p. 18). Whereas the act of speaking for others denies those others the right to be the subjects of their own speech, the refusal to speak on behalf of the oppressed, conversely, assumes that they are in a position to act as such fully empowered subjects.

Alcoff's argument here follows closely that of Gayatri Spivak in 'Can the Subaltern Speak?',[43] where, taking issue with Foucault and Deleuze's influential remarks on the 'fundamental . . . indignity of speaking for others',[44] she argues that any invocation of the oppressed as self-representing and 'fully in control of the knowledge of their own oppression' (p. 274) serves to effect a double concealment: on the one hand, of the fact that these self-representing oppressed are still (since they are *invoked* to play a role) a fact of discourse, a representation; and, on the other, of the role of intellectuals in constructing this self-negating representation, their representation of themselves as transparent. There can be no simple refusal of the role of judge or of universal witness, since to do so is to denegate the institutional conditions, consequences, and responsibilities of intellectual work.[45]

The particular circumstances under which it is appropriate or inappropriate to represent the interests of others, and to attempt to bracket off one's own interests in the process, are of course always complex and contingent; precisely because of the complexity of the category of position. What Alcoff's

[43] Gayatri Chakravorty Spivak, 'Can the Subaltern Speak?', in Cary Nelson and Lawrence Grossberg (eds.), *Marxism and the Interpretation of Culture* (Urbana: University of Illinois Press, 1988), 271–313.

[44] 'Intellectuals and Power: A Conversation Between Michel Foucault and Gilles Deleuze', in Michel Foucault, *Language, Counter-Memory, Practice*, trans. Donald F. Bouchard and Sherry Simon (Ithaca, NY: Cornell University Press, 1977), 209.

[45] Elsewhere Spivak writes: 'The position that only the subaltern can know the subaltern, only women can know women, and so on, cannot be held as a theoretical presupposition . . . for it predicates the possibility of knowledge on identity.' Gayatri Chakravorty Spivak, 'A Literary Representation of the Subaltern: A Woman's Text from the Third World', *In Other Worlds: Essays in Cultural Politics* (New York and London: Methuen, 1987), 253–4.

argument usefully does, however, is move away from a naïve realism of social positionality towards a more differentiated politics of enunciation.

The problem with tying an utterance to social position or social 'identity' is that the latter tends to act as (or to be taken as) something fully external to discourse, the place of the Real *as against* the discursive. But position and identity are discursively realized and imagined; and they are shifting and multiple. Speaking positions, and the authority (or lack of it) that accompanies them, are, however, powerful and very real performative *effects*. By this I mean that they are the effects of discursive institutions of authorization which selectively credit the speaker with membership of one or more speech communities and with a place on one or more hierarchies of authority and credibility. They are not effects, that is to say, of 'objective' social position, but of an imputed position; they are moments of a semiotic politics, not reflections of a political reality that takes place elsewhere.[46]

There is no point of leverage *outside* the politics of representation, only an endless and unequal negotiation of relations of power within it (and within its institutions, which are largely controlled but not owned by the knowledge class). The determinations operating on the rights of 'cultural' intellectuals to speak for others are twofold, and pull in contradictory directions. The first (an enabling condition) is the 'uneasiness' of the relation between group and speaker, the slight but significant detachment of speaking position from *representation* of a speech community (in the sense of standing for it, sharing its characteristics).[47] I have used the

---

[46] I elaborate some of the political aspects of the distinction between knowing and being supposed to know in 'Discipline and Discipleship', *Textual Practice*, 2: 3 (1988), 307–23.

[47] Cf. the discussion by Boltanski and Thévenot of the procedures by which structures of typicality (generality) are constructed: Luc Boltanski and Laurent Thévenot, *De la justification: Les Économies de la grandeur* (Paris: Gallimard, 1991). Cf. also John Guillory's argument in *Cultural Capital* (pp. 6–7) that the politics of canon critique has operated as a kind of displacement of the liberal-pluralist politics of representation. The assumption it makes is that of a 'homology between the process of *exclusion*, by which socially defined minorities are excluded from the exercise of power or from political representation, and the

concept of regime of value to theorize this partial detachment. Like the infinitesimal swerve of Lucretius's atoms, it is this gap that allows the universe of discourse to be at once rule-governed and open-ended. The second determination is their membership of a social class with real, though ambivalent, class interests in the implementation of modernity. The privileged possession of cultural capital translates into an exercise of power that can well take the form of an apparent self-negation or self-abasement.

'Culture is our specific capital', says Bourdieu, 'and, even in the most radical probing, we tend to forget the true foundation of our specific power, of the particular form of domination we exercise.'[48] In seeking to place the work of cultural intellectuals in the framework of a class formation and a set of more or less definite class interests, I have sought to make this work less transparent, and so to take seriously the ways in which it might further the knowledge class's own interests rather than those of the groups for whom intellectuals claim to speak, or any more universal interest.

One response to this shift towards the interests of intellectual work might be simply to condemn those interests, to find them irrelevant to the real stakes in social struggle; but if it is true that intellectual work is indeed structured by a specific (if ambivalent) social interest, then such a response can only miss the point (and indeed can only be made from within the structure of interest that it denounces). A different kind of response might be to give serious attention—as Gouldner, for example, does—to the progressive political potential of the knowledge class. In Gouldner's analysis, the political interests of the New Class are defined by its revolutionizing relation to the mode of

process of *selection*, by which certain works are designated canonical, others noncanonical. . . . Canonical and noncanonical authors are supposed to *stand for* particular social groups, dominant or subordinate.' This is, in all senses of the word, an *imaginary* politics; it relies on an essentialist conception of social 'identity' and it misrecognizes the specific location of the canon (and its critique) in the institution of the school.

[48] Bourdieu, *In Other Words*, 107.

production (the modernizing imperative to 'make it new') and its ambivalent relation to the classes above and beneath it. In the advanced industrial economies it serves as 'a technical intelligentsia whose work is subordinate to the old moneyed class. The New Class is useful to the old for the technical services it performs and, also, to legitimate the society as modern and scientific.'[49] As its effective control over production grows, however, so does its political power *vis-à-vis* the bourgeoisie. In the political sphere proper, it is only through the New Class that the old dominant class can exercise an influence on state policy, and 'as the organizational units of the economy and state become larger and more bureaucratic, the survival and control of the old class becomes more attenuated, more indirect, ever more dependent on the intelligentsia of the New Class' (p. 50). In terms both of its relation to the mode of production and its relation to the bourgeoisie, then, the New Class is an inherently progressive political force, and indeed is 'a centre of whatever human emancipation is possible in the foreseeable future' (p. 83). It neither restricts the forces of production nor develops them only in so far as they are profitable; in its commitment to an ideal of freedom of knowledge it embodies a rationality which is broader than the merely instrumental; it is internationalist and cosmopolitan; and by extension—this is perhaps the most dated aspect of Gouldner's argument—its politics are logically left-wing.

A strong form of this thesis can be found in a recent essay of Pierre Bourdieu's which uncharacteristically abandons the sceptical detachment of the sociologist in order to argue directly for the necessity of a corporatist politics of intellectuals.[50] At its most basic, this is an argument that intellectuals should recognize their right to 'accord themselves what every other group accords itself, i.e., the right to publicly defend their vision of the world, as particular and self-

[49] Gouldner, *The Future of Intellectuals and the Rise of the New Class*, 11–12.
[50] Pierre Bourdieu, 'The Corporatism of the Universal: The Role of Intellectuals in the Modern World', trans. Carolyn Betensky, *Telos*, 81 (Fall 1989), 99–110; further references are given in the text.

interested as it might be' (p. 110). In particular, they should accord themselves the right to defend the autonomy of intellectual work against the various powerful threats to it: threats to funding, to working conditions, to the right to autonomy both from commercial pressures and from political direction of the goals of research, threats to the right to disseminate knowledge in the public domain, and indeed to the concept of a public domain itself. Despite compelling reasons, intellectuals have not usually been adept at such self-defence: they

have often emphasized the defence of major universal causes and rejected the defence of their own interests as merely corporatist, forgetting that the defence of the universal presupposes the defence of the defenders of the universal. . . . They can do this without remorse or moral hesitation since, by defending themselves as a whole, they defend the universal.   (p. 103)

What this universal might be is never spelled out precisely, but, as with Gouldner's conception of the culture of critical discourse that characterizes the New Class of intellectuals, it seems to be grounded in the first instance in the norms and protocols of scientific work; in the free dissemination of scientific knowledge; and in the fact that intellectual work is formed in the rejection of particularisms. It is contrasted to commercially oriented research, to the bureaucratic regulation of knowledge, and to journalism.

The claim that Bourdieu makes is not precisely that intellectuals represent a universal class, since they 'have not escaped the universal temptation to universalize their particular interests' (p. 109). There are, however, two reasons why they are capable of a certain kind of class generosity. The first is 'their situation as dominated dominators or, more precisely, as dominated parties within the field of power—a situation which leads them to feel solidarity with any and all the dominated, despite the fact that, being in possession of one of the major means of domination, cultural capital, they partake of the dominant order' (ibid.). The other is the capacity for self-reflexivity given by intellectual work (for example, sociology), and thus their awareness of 'the *privileges* underlying their claims to the universal' (p. 110). The politics of intellectuals will be a 'corporatism of the universal' to the extent that it seeks to universalize the privileged conditions of their own existence.

What this argument promises is a way out of that politics of the alibi whereby intellectuals claim the right to speak from a position of relative power on behalf of the powerless and the dispossessed. It is, however, a wrong argument. It relies for all its force on a distinction between 'real' intellectuals and 'pseudo-' intellectuals (the treacherous clerks within the disciplines, the bureaucrats and journalists without); but this distinction is impossible to maintain without at the same time destroying any notion of the possible unity of the class fraction of intellectuals. Like so many other accounts of the intelligentsia, it massively overestimates the social value of intellectual work. And it discards all of that elementary suspicion that causes Gouldner to describe the New Class of intellectuals as a *'flawed* universal class'—flawed in the sense that its interests do not coincide with those of other social classes.[51] The alternative to the claim to the disinterestedness of the knowledge class[52] is not simply that it should commit itself to the defence of its own class interests. As Bourdieu himself has made abundantly clear, cultural capital is always at best a partial good: at once an instrument of knowing (and in that sense *potentially* universal), and an instrument of class distinction.

To say that we must be as suspicious of the interests of intellectuals as we are of any other social interests is not to imply that we should or somehow could reject them. To the contrary: we can act in good faith only as long as we recognize that there is no escape from the consequences of

[51] Gouldner, *The Future of Intellectuals*, 83.

[52] The *locus classicus* for this claim is Mannheim's description of the *freischwebende Intelligenz* (Max Weber's term) as 'a relatively classless stratum'. Karl Mannheim, *Ideology and Utopia: An Introduction to the Sociology of Knowledge*, trans. Louis Wirth and Edward Shils (New York: Harvest, 1936), 155 ff.

possession of cultural capital, just as there is no way of getting outside the game of value judgement and the game of cultural distinction. At the same time, this structure of interest means that it is politically crucial for intellectuals not to universalize the competences they possess as norms which can be used to totalize the cultural field.

The question of our relation to regimes of value is not a personal but an institutional question. A key condition of any institutional politics, however, is that intellectuals do not denegate their own status as possessors of cultural capital; that they accept and struggle with the contradictions that this entails; and that their cultural politics, right across the spectrum of cultural texts, should be openly and without embarrassment presented as their politics, not someone else's.

List of Works Cited

ABERCROMBIE, NICHOLAS, and URRY, JOHN, *Capital, Labour and the Middle Classes* (London: Allen and Unwin, 1983).

AITKIN, DON, *Stability and Change in Australian Politics*, 2nd edn. (Canberra: ANU Press, 1982).

ALCOFF, LINDA, 'The Problem of Speaking for Others', *Cultural Critique*, 20 (1991–2), 5–32.

APPADURAI, ARJUN, 'Introduction: Commodities and the Politics of Value', in *The Social Life of Things: Commodities in Cultural Perspective*, ed. Arjun Appadurai (Cambridge: Cambridge University Press, 1986), 3–63.

ARMSTRONG, NANCY, and TENNENHOUSE, LEONARD, *The Imaginary Puritan: Literature, Intellectual Labour, and the Origins of Personal Life* (Berkeley: University of California Press, 1992).

ASHBOLT, ANTHONY, 'Against Left Optimism: A Reply to John Docker', *Arena*, 61 (1982), 132–40.

BALIBAR, ÉTIENNE, and WALLERSTEIN, IMMANUEL, *Race, Nation, Class: Ambiguous Identities* (London: Verso, 1991).

BAUMAN, ZYGMUNT, *Legislators and Interpreters: On Modernity, Postmodernity and Intellectuals* (Cambridge: Polity Press, 1987).

BAXTER, JANEEN, EMMISON, MICHAEL, and WESTERN, JOHN, *Class Analysis and Contemporary Australia* (Melbourne: Macmillan, 1991).

BECHHOFER, FRANK, and ELLIOTT, BRIAN, 'Petty Property: The Survival of a Moral Economy', in *The Petite Bourgeoisie: Comparative Studies of the Uneasy Stratum*, ed. Frank Bechhofer and Brian Elliott (New York: St Martin's Press, 1981), 182–200.

BELL, DANIEL, *The Coming of Postindustrial Society: A Venture in Social Forecasting* (New York: Basic Books, 1973).

BENNETT, TONY, 'Introduction: Popular Culture and "the Turn to Gramsci"', in *Popular Culture and Social Relations*, ed. Tony Bennett, Colin Mercer, and Janet Woollacott (Milton Keynes: Open University Press, 1986), pp. xi–xix.

—— 'Marxist Cultural Politics: In Search of "the Popular"', *Australian Journal of Cultural Studies*, 1: 2 (1983), 2–28.

—— *Outside Literature* (London: Routledge, 1990).

—— 'The Politics of "the Popular" and Popular Culture', in *Popular Culture and Social Relations*, ed. Tony Bennett, Colin Mercer, and

Janet Woollacott (Milton Keynes: Open University Press, 1986), 6–21.

—— 'Texts in History: The Determinations of Readings and Their Texts', *Journal of the Midwest Modern Language Association*, 18: 1 (1985), 1–16.

—— and WOOLLACOTT, JANET, *Bond and Beyond: The Political Career of a Popular Hero* (London and New York: Methuen, 1987).

BENNINGTON, GEOFF, *Lyotard: Writing the Event* (Manchester: Manchester University Press, 1988).

BHABHA, HOMI, *The Location of Culture* (London and New York: Routledge, 1994).

BOLTANSKI, LUC, and THÉVENOT, LAURENT, *De la justification: Les Économies de la grandeur* (Paris: Gallimard, 1991).

BOURDIEU, PIERRE, *Ce que parler veut dire: L'Économie des échanges linguistiques* (Paris: Fayard, 1981).

—— 'The Corporatism of the Universal: The Role of Intellectuals in the Modern World', trans. Carolyn Betensky, *Telos*, 81 (1989), 99–110.

—— *Distinction: A Social Critique of the Judgment of Taste*, trans. Richard Nice (Cambridge, Mass.: Harvard University Press, 1984).

—— 'The Forms of Capital', in *Handbook of Theory and Research for the Sociology of Education*, ed. John G. Richardson (New York: Greenwood, 1986), 241–58.

—— 'Les Fractions de la classe dominante et les modes d'appropriation des œuvres d'art', *Information sur les sciences sociales*, 13: 3 (1974), 7–31.

—— *In Other Words: Essays Towards a Reflexive Sociology*, trans. Matthew Adamson (Stanford, Calif.: Stanford University Press, 1990).

—— 'Intellectual Field and Creative Project', in *Knowledge and Control: New Directions for the Sociology of Education*, ed. M. Young (London: Collier Macmillan, 1971), 161–88.

—— *Outline of a Theory of Practice*, trans. Richard Nice (Cambridge: Cambridge University Press, 1977).

—— 'The Specificity of the Scientific Field and the Social Conditions of the Progress of Reason', *Social Science Information*, 14: 4 (1975), 19–47.

—— 'Sur l'objectivation participante', *Actes de la recherche en sciences sociales*, 23 (Sept. 1978), 67–9.

—— 'What Makes a Social Class? On the Theoretical and Practical Existence of Groups', *Berkeley Journal of Sociology*, XXXII (1987), 1–17.

—— and DARBEL, ALAIN, *L'Amour de l'art: Les Musées d'art européens et leur public*, 2nd rev. edn. (Paris: Minuit, 1969).

BOURDIEU, PIERRE, and PASSERON, J.-C., *Reproduction in Education, Society and Culture*, trans. Richard Nice (London: Sage, 1977).

—— BOLTANSKI, L., CASTEL, R., and CHAMBOREDON, J. -D., *Un art moyen: Essai sur les usages sociaux de la photographie* (Paris: Minuit, 1965).

BRAVERMAN, HARRY, *Labor and Monopoly Capital: The Degradation of Work in the Twentieth Century* (New York: Monthly Review Press, 1974).

BRECHT, BERTOLT, 'Against Georg Lukács', trans. Stuart Hood, *Aesthetics and Politics* (London: New Left Books, 1977).

BRUCE-BRIGGS, B. (ed.), *The New Class?* (New Brunswick, NJ: Transaction Press, 1979).

BRUNSDON, CHARLOTTE, 'Problems with Quality', *Screen*, 31: 1 (1990), 67–90.

BÜRGER, CHRISTA, 'The Disappearance of Art: The Postmodernism Debate in the US', *Telos*, 68 (Summer 1986), 93–106.

—— 'Einleitung: Die Dichotomie von hoher und niederer Literatur. Eine Problemskizze', in *Zur Dichotomisierung von hoher und niederer Literatur*, ed. Christa Bürger, Peter Bürger, and Jochen Schulte-Sasse (Frankfurt am Main: Suhrkamp, 1982).

BÜRGER, PETER, *Theory of the Avant-Garde*, trans. Michael Shaw, Foreword by Jochen Schulte-Sasse, Theory and History of Literature, Vol. 4 (Minneapolis: University of Minnesota Press, 1984).

BURKE, PETER, 'The "Discovery" of Popular Culture', in *People's History and Socialist Theory*, ed. Raphael Samuel, History Workshop Series (London: Routledge, 1981), 216–26.

BURNHAM, JAMES, *The Managerial Revolution: What is Happening in the World* (New York: John Day, 1941).

BURRIS, VAL, 'Class Structure and Political Ideology', *The Insurgent Sociologist*, 14: 2 (1987), 5–46.

BUTLER, JUDITH, *Gender Trouble: Feminism and the Subversion of Identity* (New York and London: Routledge, 1990).

CALLINICOS, ALEX, 'The "New Middle Class" and Socialist Politics', *International Socialism*, 2: 20 (1983), 82–119.

CARCHEDI, GUGLIELMO, *On the Economic Identification of Social Classes* (London: Routledge, 1977).

CHAMBERS, IAIN, *Popular Culture: The Metropolitan Experience* (London: Methuen, 1986).

CLARKE, JOHN, HALL, STUART, JEFFERSON, TONY, and ROBERTS, BRIAN, 'Subcultures, Cultures and Class: A Theoretical Overview', in *Resistance through Rituals: Youth Subcultures in Post-War Britain*, ed. Stuart Hall and Tony Jefferson (London: Harper-Collins, 1976).

CLIFFORD, JAMES, 'Introduction: Partial Truths', in *Writing Culture: The Poetics and Politics of Ethnography*, ed. James Clifford and George E. Marcus (Berkeley: University of California Press, 1986), 1–26.

—— *The Predicament of Culture: Twentieth-Century Ethnography, Literature, and Art* (Cambridge, Mass.: Harvard University Press, 1988).

—— and MARCUS, GEORGE E. (eds.), *Writing Culture: The Poetics and Politics of Ethnography* (Berkeley: University of California Press, 1986).

COHEN, PHIL, 'Subcultural Conflict and Working-Class Community', in *Culture, Media, Language: Working Papers in Cultural Studies, 1972–79*, ed. Stuart Hall *et al.* (London: Hutchinson, 1980).

COLLINS, JIM, *Uncommon Cultures: Popular Culture and Post-Modernism* (New York and London: Routledge, 1989).

COLLINS, RANDALL, *The Credential Society: An Historical Sociology of Education and Stratification* (New York: Academic Press, 1979).

CONNELL, R. W., *Which Way is Up? Essays on Class, Sex and Culture* (Sydney: Allen and Unwin, 1983).

CONNOR, STEVEN, 'The Modern and the Postmodern as History', *Essays in Criticism*, XXXVII: 3 (1987), 181–92.

—— *Postmodernist Culture: An Introduction to Theories of the Contemporary* (Oxford: Basil Blackwell, 1989).

—— *Theory and Cultural Value* (Oxford: Basil Blackwell, 1992).

D'ALBA, RICHARD, *Ethnic Identity: The Transformation of White America* (New Haven, Conn.: Yale University Press, 1990).

DAHRENDORF, RALF, *Soziale Klassen und Klassenkonflikt* (Stuttgart, 1957).

DE CERTEAU, MICHEL, *L'Écriture de l'histoire* (Paris: Gallimard, 1978).

—— *Heterologies: Discourse on the Other*, trans. Brian Massumi, Theory and History of Literature, Vol. 17 (Minneapolis: University of Minnesota Press, 1986).

—— 'La Lecture absolue (Théorie et pratique des mystiques chrétiens: XVIe–XVIIe siècles)', in *Problèmes actuels de la lecture*, ed. Lucien Dällenbach and Jean Ricardou, Colloques de Cérisy (Paris: Clancier-Guénaud, 1982), 65–80.

—— *The Practice of Everyday Life*, trans. Steven Rendall (Berkeley: University of California Press, 1984).

—— JULIA, DOMINIQUE, and REVEL, JACQUES, *Une politique de la langue: La Révolution française et les patois: L'Enquête de Grégoire* (Paris: Gallimard, 1975).

DJILAS, MILOVAN, *The New Class: An Analysis of the Communist System* (New York: Praeger, 1957).

174   LIST OF WORKS CITED

DOCKER, JOHN, 'Give Them Facts — the Modern Gradgrinds', *Media Information Australia*, 30 (1983), 3–7.
—— 'In Defence of Popular Culture', *Arena*, 60 (1982), 72–87.
ECO, UMBERTO, 'Innovation and Repetition: Between Modern and Post-Modern Aesthetics', *Daedalus*, 114: 4 (1985), 161–84.
EHRENREICH, BARBARA and JOHN, 'The Professional-Managerial Class', in *Between Labor and Capital*, ed. Pat Walker (Boston: South End Press, 1979), 5–45.
FABIAN, JOHANNES, *Time and the Other: How Anthropology Makes Its Object* (New York: Columbia University Press, 1983).
FEATHERSTONE, MIKE, *Consumer Culture and Postmodernism* (London: Sage, 1991).
FEKETE, JOHN, 'Introductory Notes for a Postmodern Value Agenda', *Life After Postmodernism: Essays on Value and Culture*, ed. John Fekete (New York: St Martin's Press, 1987), pp. i-xix.
FISKE, JOHN, 'Critical Response: Meaningful Moments', *Critical Studies in Mass Communication* (Sept. 1988), 246–50.
—— 'Ethnosemiotics: Some Personal and Theoretical Reflections', *Cultural Studies*, 4: 1 (1990), 85–99.
—— *Power Plays, Power Works* (London: Verso, 1993).
—— *Understanding Popular Culture* (Boston: Unwin Hyman, 1989).
FLAUBERT, GUSTAVE, *Sentimental Education*, trans. Robert Baldick (Harmondsworth: Penguin, 1964).
FOUCAULT, MICHEL, *The Foucault Effect: Studies in Governmentality, with Two Lectures by and an Interview with Michel Foucault*, ed. Graham Burchell, Colin Gordon, and Peter Miller (Chicago: University of Chicago Press, 1991).
—— and DELEUZE, GILLES, 'Intellectuals and Power: A Conversation Between Michel Foucault and Gilles Deleuze', *Language, Counter-Memory, Practice*, trans. Donald F. Bouchard and Sherry Simon (Ithaca, NY: Cornell University Press, 1977), 205–17.
FRITH, SIMON, 'The Cultural Study of Popular Music', in *Cultural Studies*, ed. Lawrence Grossberg, Cary Nelson, and Paula Treichler (New York: Routledge, 1992), 174–86.
—— 'The Good, the Bad, and the Indifferent: Defending Popular Culture from the Populists', *Diacritics*, 21: 4 (1991), 102–15.
—— 'Hearing Secret Harmonies', in *High Theory/Low Culture: Analysing Popular Television and Film*, ed. Colin MacCabe (New York: St Martin's Press, 1986), 53–70.
FROW, JOHN, 'Discipline and Discipleship', *Textual Practice*, 2: 3 (1988), 307–23.
—— *Marxism and Literary History* (Cambridge, Mass. and Oxford: Harvard University Press and Basil Blackwell, 1986).

—— and MORRIS, MEAGHAN (eds.), *Australian Cultural Studies: A Reader* (Sydney: Allen and Unwin, 1993).

GAME, ANN, and PRINGLE, ROSEMARY, *Gender at Work* (Sydney: Allen and Unwin, 1983).

GANS, HERBERT, *Popular Culture and High Culture: An Analysis and Evaluation of Taste* (New York: Basic Books, 1974).

GARFINKEL, HAROLD, *Studies in Ethnomethodology* (New Jersey: Prentice Hall, 1967).

GARNHAM, NICHOLAS, and WILLIAMS, RAYMOND, 'Pierre Bourdieu and the Sociology of Culture', *Media, Culture and Society*, 23: 3 (1980), 209–23.

GEERTZ, CLIFFORD, *Works and Lives: The Anthropologist as Author* (Stanford, Calif.: Stanford University Press, 1988).

GENG, J.-M., *L'Illustre Inconnu* (Paris: Union Générale d'Éditions 10/18, 1978).

GIDDENS, ANTHONY, *The Class Structure of the Advanced Societies* (1973; New York: Harper and Row, 1975).

GILROY, PAUL, *'There Ain't No Black in the Union Jack': The Cultural Politics of Race and Nation* (London: Hutchinson, 1987).

GOLDTHORPE, JOHN, 'On the Service Class, Its Formation and Future', in *Social Class and the Division of Labour: Essays in Honour of Ilya Neustadt*, ed. Anthony Giddens and Gavin Mackenzie (Cambridge: Cambridge University Press, 1982), 162–85.

GORZ, ANDRÉ, *Farewell to the Working Class: An Essay on Post-Industrial Socialism*, trans. Michael Sonenscher (Boston: South End Press, 1982).

GOULDNER, ALVIN W., *The Future of Intellectuals and the Rise of the New Class: A Frame of Reference, Theses, Conjectures, Arguments and an Historical Perspective on the Role of Intellectuals and Intelligentsia in the International Class Contest of the Modern Era* (New York: Oxford University Press, 1979).

GRAFF, GERALD, *Beyond the Culture Wars: How Teaching the Conflicts Can Revitalize American Education* (New York: W. W. Norton, 1993).

GRAMSCI, ANTONIO, *Selections from the Prison Notebooks*, ed. and trans. Quintin Hoare and Geoffrey Nowell-Smith (London: Lawrence and Wishart, 1971).

GRIPSRUD, JOSTEIN, '"High Culture" Revisited', *Cultural Studies*, 3: 2 (1989), 194–207.

GROSSBERG, LAWRENCE, 'The Context of Audiences and the Politics of Difference', *Australian Journal of Communication*, 16 (1989), 13–35.

—— 'Wandering Audiences, Nomadic Critics', *Cultural Studies*, 2: 3 (1988), 377–91.

GUILLORY, JOHN, *Cultural Capital: The Problem of Literary Canon Formation* (Chicago: University of Chicago Press, 1993).

HAGSTROM, INGRID, 'Popular Culture Undefined', *Arena*, 61 (1982), 141–8.

HALL, STUART, 'Cultural Studies and its Theoretical Legacies', in *Cultural Studies*, ed. Lawrence Grossberg, Cary Nelson, and Paula Treichler (New York: Routledge, 1992), 277–94.

—— 'Notes on Deconstructing "the Popular"', in *People's History and Socialist Theory*, ed. Raphael Samuel, History Workshop Series (London: Routledge, 1981), 227–40.

HARTLEY, JOHN, 'Invisible Fictions: Television Audiences, Paedocracy, Pleasure', *Textual Practice*, 1: 2 (1987), 121–38.

—— 'The Real World of Audiences', *Critical Studies in Mass Communication* (Sept. 1988), 234–8.

—— *Tele-ology: Studies in Television* (London: Routledge, 1992).

HARVEY, DAVID, *The Condition of Postmodernity: An Enquiry Into the Origins of Cultural Change* (Oxford: Basil Blackwell, 1989).

HEBDIGE, DICK, *Hiding in the Light: On Images and Things* (London and New York: Routledge/Comedia, 1988).

—— *Subculture: The Meaning of Style* (London: Methuen, 1979).

HINDESS, BARRY, *Politics and Class Analysis* (Oxford: Basil Blackwell, 1987).

HIRST, PAUL, 'Economic Classes and Politics', in *Class and Class Structure*, ed. Alan Hunt (London: Lawrence and Wishart, 1977), 125–54.

HODGE, BOB, and McHOUL, ALEC, 'The Politics of Text and Commentary', *Textual Practice*, 6: 2 (1992), 189–209.

HUNTER, IAN, *Culture and Government: The Emergence of Literary Education* (London: Macmillan, 1988).

—— 'Setting Limits to Culture', *New Formations*, 4 (1988), 103–23.

HUYSSEN, ANDREAS, *After the Great Divide: Modernism, Mass Culture, Postmodernism* (Bloomington: Indiana University Press, 1986).

JAMESON, FREDRIC, 'On "Cultural Studies"', *Social Text*, 34 (1993), 17–52.

—— 'Reification and Utopia in Mass Culture', *Social Text*, 1 (1979), 130–48.

JAMOUS, H., and PELOILLE, B., 'Changes in the French University-Hospital System', in *Professions and Professionalization*, ed. J. A. Jackson, Sociological Studies, 3 (Cambridge: Cambridge University Press, 1970), 111–52.

JANIK, ALLEN, and TOULMIN, STEPHEN, *Wittgenstein's Vienna* (New York: Simon and Schuster, 1973).

JONES, GARETH STEDMAN, *Languages of Class: Studies in English Working Class History, 1832–1982* (Cambridge: Cambridge University Press, 1983).

KING, NOEL, and ROWSE, TIM, '"Typical Aussies": Television and Populism in Australia', *Framework*, 22–3 (Autumn 1983), 37–42.

KODAMA, FUKIO, 'How Investment Decisions Are Made in Japanese Industry', in *The Evaluation of Scientific Research*, ed. D. Evered and S. Harnett (London: J. Wiley, 1987), 201–14.

KONRAD, GYORGY, and SZELENYI, IVAN, *The Intellectuals on the Road to Class Power*, trans. Andrew Arato and Richard C. Allen (Brighton: Harvester, 1978).

KOSÍK, KAREL, *Die Dialektik des Konkreten: Eine Studie zur Problematik des Menschen und der Welt*, trans. Marianne Hoffmann (Frankfurt am Main: Suhrkamp, 1967).

KRISTEVA, JULIA, 'Women's Time', *The Kristeva Reader*, ed. Toril Moi (Oxford: Basil Blackwell, 1986), 187–213.

KUHN, ANNETTE, and WOLPE, ANNMARIE, 'Introduction', in *Feminism and Materialism: Women and Modes of Production*, ed. Annette Kuhn and AnnMarie Wolpe (London: Routledge and Kegan Paul, 1978), 1–10.

LACLAU, ERNESTO, *New Reflections on the Revolution of Our Time* (London: Verso, 1990).

—— *Politics and Ideology in Marxist Theory: Capitalism — Fascism — Populism* (London: Verso, 1977).

—— 'Populist Rupture and Discourse', *Screen Education*, 34 (1980), 89–93.

—— '"Socialism", the "People", "Democracy": The Transformation of Hegemonic Logic', *Social Text*, 7 (Spring/Summer 1983), 115–19.

—— and MOUFFE, CHANTAL, *Hegemony and Socialist Strategy: Towards a Radical Democratic Politics*, trans. Winston Moore and Paul Cammack (London: Verso, 1985).

—— 'Recasting Marxism: Hegemony and New Political Movements', Interview, *Socialist Review*, 12: 6 (1982), 91–113.

LASH, SCOTT, *Sociology of Postmodernism* (London: Routledge, 1990).

—— and URRY JOHN, *The End of Organized Capitalism* (Cambridge: Polity Press, 1987).

LITTEK, WOLFGANG, and HEISIG, ULRICH, 'Work Organization under Technological Change: Sources of Differentiation and the Reproduction of Social Inequality in Processes of Change', in *Organization Theory and Class Analysis: New Approaches and New Issues*, ed. Stewart R. Clegg (Berlin and New York: Walter de Gruyter, 1990), 299–314.

LOTMAN, JURIJ, *The Structure of the Artistic Text*, trans. Ronald Vroon, Michigan Slavic Contributions, No. 7 (Ann Arbor: University of Michigan, 1977).

LUKÁCS, GEORG, *Soul and Form*, trans. Anna Bostock (Cambridge, Mass.: MIT Press, 1974).

LYONS, PAUL, 'Yuppie: A Contemporary American Keyword', *Socialist Review*, 19: 1 (1989), 111–22.

LYOTARD, JEAN-FRANÇOIS, *The Differend: Phrases in Dispute*, trans. Georges Van Den Abbeele, Theory and History of Literature, Vol. 46 (Minneapolis: University of Minnesota Press, 1988).

—— *The Post-Modern Condition: A Report on Knowledge*, trans. Geoff Bennington and Brian Massumi, Theory and History of Literature, Vol. 10 (Minneapolis: University of Minnesota Press, 1984).

—— 'Rules and Paradoxes and Svelte Appendix', trans. Brian Massumi, *Cultural Critique*, 5 (1986–7), 209–19.

—— and THÉBAUD, JEAN-LOUP, *Just Gaming*, trans. Wlad Godzich, Theory and History of Literature, Vol. 20 (Minneapolis: University of Minnesota Press, 1985).

MACHLUP, FRITZ, *The Branches of Learning* (Princeton, NJ: Princeton University Press, 1982).

—— *The Economics of Information and Human Capital* (Princeton, NJ: Princeton University Press, 1984).

—— *Knowledge and Knowledge Production* (Princeton, NJ: Princeton University Press, 1980).

—— *The Production and Distribution of Knowledge in the United States* (Princeton, NJ: Princeton University Press, 1962).

McROBBIE, ANGELA, 'Dance and Social Fantasy', in *Gender and Generation*, ed. Angela McRobbie and Mica Nava (London: Macmillan, 1984), 130–61.

—— 'Settling Accounts with Subcultures: A Feminist Critique', *Screen Education*, 34 (1980), 37–49.

MALLET, SERGE, *La Nouvelle Classe ouvrière* (Paris: Seuil, 1963).

MANNHEIM, KARL, *Ideology and Utopia: An Introduction to the Sociology of Knowledge*, trans. Louis Wirth and Edward Shils (New York: Harvest-Harcourt, Brace and World, 1936).

MARCUS, GEORGE E., and FISCHER, MICHAEL M. J. (eds.), *Anthropology as Cultural Critique: An Experimental Moment in the Human Sciences* (Chicago: University of Chicago Press, 1986).

MARX, KARL, *Grundrisse: Foundations of the Critique of Political Economy (Rough Draft)*, trans. and foreword by Martin Nicolaus (Harmondsworth: Penguin, 1973).

MENSCH, BETTY, 'Freedom of Contract as Ideology', *Stanford Law Review*, 33 (1981), 753–72.

MICHAELS, ERIC, 'Bad Aboriginal Art', *Art and Text*, 28 (1988), 59–73.

MORLEY, DAVID, *The 'Nationwide' Audience: Structure and Decoding* (London: BFI, 1980).

—— *Television Audiences and Cultural Studies* (London: Routledge, 1992).

MORRIS, MEAGHAN, 'At Henry Parkes Motel', *Cultural Studies*, 2: 1 (1988), 1–47.

—— 'Banality in Cultural Studies', *Discourse*, X: 2 (1988), 3–29.

MORSE, MARGARET, 'An Ontology of Everyday Distraction: The Freeway, the Mall, and Television', in *Logics of Television: Essays in Cultural Criticism*, ed. Patricia Mellencamp (Bloomington: Indiana University Press, 1990), 193–221.

NIGHTINGALE, VIRGINIA, 'What's "Ethnographic" about Ethnographic Audience Research?', *Australian Journal of Communication*, 16 (1989), 50–63.

NOBLE, D., *America by Design* (New York: Oxford University Press, 1979).

NOVE, ALEC, 'Is There a Ruling Class in the USSR?', in *Classes, Power and Conflict*, ed. Anthony Giddens and David Held (London: Macmillan, 1982), 588–604.

NOWELL-SMITH, GEOFFREY, 'Popular Culture', *New Formations*, 2 (1987), 79–90.

OFFE, CLAUS, *Disorganized Capitalism: Contemporary Transformations of Work and Politics*, ed. John Keane (Cambridge: Polity Press, 1985).

PÊCHEUX, MICHEL, *Les Vérités de la Palice* (Paris: Maspéro, 1975).

PERKIN, HAROLD, *The Rise of Professional Society: England Since 1880* (London and New York: Routledge, 1989).

PFEIL, FRED, *Another Tale to Tell: Politics and Narrative in Postmodern Culture* (London: Verso, 1990).

POLLACK, FREDERICK, 'Theses on Intellectuals', *Representations*, 39 (Summer 1992), 71–9.

POOVEY, MARY, 'Aesthetics and Political Economy in the Eighteenth Century', in *Aesthetics and Ideology*, ed. George Levine and Carolyn Williams (New Brunswick, NJ: Rutgers University Press, forthcoming).

POPULAR MEMORY GROUP, 'Popular Memory: Theory, Politics, Method', in *Making Histories: Studies in History-Writing and Politics*, ed. Richard Johnson *et al.* (Minneapolis: University of Minnesota Press, 1982), 205–52.

PORAT, MARC URI, *The Information Economy*, Special Publication 77–12, 9 vols. (Washington, DC: Office of Telecommunications, 1977).

POULANTZAS, NICOS, *Classes in Contemporary Capitalism*, trans. David Fernbach (London: Verso, 1975).

PRZEWORSKI, ADAM, *Capitalism and Social Democracy* (Cambridge: Cambridge University Press, 1985).

—— 'Class, Production and Politics: A Reply to Burawoy', *Socialist Review*, 19: 2 (1989), 87–111.

—— *Democracy and the Market: Political and Economic Reforms in Eastern Europe and Latin America* (Cambridge: Cambridge University Press, 1991).

—— 'Material Interests, Class Compromise, and the Transition to Socialism', *Politics and Society*, 10: 2 (1980), 125–53.

—— 'Proletariat into a Class: The Process of Class Formation from Karl Kautsky's *The Class Struggle* to Recent Controversies', *Politics and Society*, 7: 4 (1977), 343–401.

RADNOTI, SANDOR, 'Mass Culture', *Telos*, 48 (Summer 1981), 27–47.

RADWAY, JANICE, *Reading the Romance: Women, Patriarchy, and Popular Literature* (Chapel Hill: University of North Carolina Press, 1984).

—— 'Reception Study: Ethnography and the Problems of Dispersed Audiences and Nomadic Subjects', *Cultural Studies*, 2: 3 (1988), 359–76.

REDHEAD, STEVE, *The End-of-the-Century Party: Youth and Pop Towards 2000* (Manchester: Manchester University Press, 1990).

RENNER, KARL, *Wandlungen der modernen Gesellschaft: Zwei Abhandlungen über die Probleme der Nachkriegzeit* (Vienna: Verlag der Wiener Volksbuchhandlung, 1953).

ROBBINS, BRUCE, *Secular Vocations: Intellectuals, Professionalism, Culture* (London and New York: Verso, 1993).

ROEDIGER, DAVID D., *The Wages of Whiteness: Race and the Making of the American Working Class* (London: Verso, 1991).

ROSS, ANDREW, *No Respect: Intellectuals and Popular Culture* (New York and London: Routledge, 1989).

ROUTH, WILLIAM, 'Keith Windschuttle's Media', *Australian Journal of Cultural Studies*, 3.1 (1985), 128–34.

ROWSE, TIM, 'Reply to John Fiske's Paper', *Continuum*, 1:2 (1988), 67–70.

—— 'The Trouble with Hegemony: Popular Culture and Multiculturalism', *Politics* (Nov. 1985), 70–6.

RUBIN, GAYLE, 'The Traffic in Women: Notes on the "Political Economy" of Sex', in *Toward an Anthropology of Women*, ed.

Rayna R. Reiter (New York and London: Monthly Review Press, 1975), 157–210.

RUBIN, MICHAEL ROGERS, and HUBER, MARY TAYLOR, *The Knowledge Industry in the United States, 1960–1980* (Princeton, NJ: Princeton University Press, 1986).

RUSTIN, MICHAEL, 'The Politics of Post-Fordism: Or, the Trouble with "New Times"', *New Left Review*, 175 (May/June 1989), 54–77.

SAHLINS, MARSHALL, *Culture and Practical Reason* (Chicago: Chicago University Press, 1976).

SAID, EDWARD, 'Representing the Colonized: Anthropology's Interlocutors', *Critical Inquiry*, 15 (1989), 205–25.

SCHIACH, MORAG, *Discourse on Popular Culture: Class, Gender and History in Cultural Analysis, 1730 to the Present* (Cambridge: Polity Press, 1987).

SCHWARZ, BILL, 'Popular Culture: The Long March', *Cultural Studies*, 3: 2 (1989), 250–5.

SENNETT, RICHARD, and COBB, JONATHAN, *The Hidden Injuries of Class*, 2nd edn. (New York: Vintage, 1973).

SLOTERDIJK, PETER, *Critique of Cynical Reason*, trans. Michael Eldred, Foreword by Andreas Huyssen, Theory and History of Literature, Vol. 40 (Minneapolis: University of Minnesota Press, 1987).

SMITH, BARBARA HERRNSTEIN, *Contingencies of Value: Alternative Perspectives for Critical Theory* (Cambridge, Mass.: Harvard University Press, 1988).

SMITH, TERRY, *Making the Modern: Industry, Art, and Design in America* (Chicago: University of Chicago Press, 1993).

SPIVAK, GAYATRI CHAKRAVORTY, 'Can the Subaltern Speak?', in *Marxism and the Interpretation of Culture*, ed. Cary Nelson and Lawrence Grossberg (Urbana: University of Illinois Press, 1988), 271–313.

—— *In Other Worlds: Essays in Cultural Politics* (New York and London: Methuen, 1987).

STEWART, SUSAN, 'Ceci Tuera Cela: Graffiti as Crime and Art', in *Life After Postmodernism: Essays on Culture and Value*, ed. John Fekete (New York: St Martin's Press, 1987), 161–80.

—— *Crimes of Writing: Problems in the Containment of Representation* (New York: Oxford University Press, 1991).

STRATHERN, MARILYN, *The Gender of the Gift: Problems with Women and Problems with Society in Melanesia* (Berkeley: University of California Press, 1988).

THOMAS, NICHOLAS, *Entangled Objects: Exchange, Material Culture, and Colonialism in the Pacific* (Cambridge, Mass.: Harvard University Press, 1991).

TURNBULL, DAVID, 'Pierre Bourdieu and the Blainey Debate', *Arena*, 74 (1986), 133–7.

UNGER, ROBERTO MANGABEIRA, *The Critical Legal Studies Movement* (Cambridge, Mass.: Harvard University Press, 1986).

URRY, JOHN, *The Tourist Gaze: Leisure and Travel in Contemporary Societies* (London: Sage, 1990).

WAGNER, ROY, *The Invention of Culture* (New Jersey: Prentice Hall, 1975).

WALLERSTEIN, IMMANUEL, 'The Bourgeois(ie) as Concept and Reality', *New Left Review*, 167 (1988), 91–106.

WEBER, SAMUEL, 'Afterword: Literature—Just Making It', in Jean-François Lyotard and Jean-Loup Thébaud, *Just Gaming*, trans. Wlad Godzich, Theory and History of Literature, Vol. 20 (Minneapolis: University of Minnesota Press, 1985), 101–20.

WESTOBY, ADAM, 'Mental Work, Education, and the Division of Labour', in *Intellectuals, Universities, and the State in Western Modern Societies*, ed. Ron Eyerman, Lennart G. Svensson, and Thomas Söderqvist (Berkeley: University of California Press, 1987), 127–53.

WILLIAMS, RAYMOND, *The Country and the City* (New York: Oxford University Press, 1973).

—— *The Long Revolution*, rev. edn. (1961; New York: Harper and Row, 1966).

—— *Marxism and Literature* (Oxford: Oxford University Press, 1977).

—— *Towards 2000* (Harmondsworth: Penguin, 1983).

WILLIS, PAUL, *Learning to Labour: How Working Class Kids Get Working Class Jobs* (Farnborough: Saxon House, 1977).

—— et al., *Common Culture: Symbolic Work at Play in the Everyday Cultures of the Young* (Milton Keynes: Open University Press, 1990).

WILLIS, SUSAN, 'Hardcore: Subculture American Style', *Critical Inquiry*, 19: 2 (1993), 365–83.

WINDSCHUTTLE, KEITH, *The Media* (Ringwood: Penguin, 1984).

WORPOLE, KEN, *Reading by Numbers: Contemporary Publishing and Popular Fiction* (London: Comedia, 1984).

WRIGHT, ERIK OLIN, *Class, Crisis and the State* (London: Verso, 1979).

—— *Classes* (London: Verso, 1985).

—— 'Intellectuals and the Class Structure of Capitalist Society', in *Between Labor and Capital*, ed. Pat Walker (Boston: South End Press, 1979), 191–211.

—— 'Rethinking, Once Again, the Concept of Class Structure', in Erik Olin Wright et al., *The Debate on Classes* (London: Verso, 1989), 269–348.

YOUNG, ROBERT, 'The Politics of "The Politics of Literary Theory"', *Oxford Literary Review*, 10 (1988), 131–57.

ZEITLIN, MAURICE, 'Corporate Ownership and Control: The Large Corporation and the Capitalist Class', in *Classes, Power, and Conflict: Classical and Contemporary Debates*, ed. Anthony Giddens and David Held (London: Macmillan, 1982), 196–223.

Index